R I D E R

Mark Rudman

RIDER

Wesleyan University Press

Published by University Press of New England

Hanover and London

Wesleyan University Press
Published by University Press of New England, Hanover, NH 03755

Printed in the United States of America
5 4 3 2 1
CIP data appear at the end of the book

Grateful acknowledgment is made to the editors of the magazines in which sections of this book first appeared: *The American Poetry Review,* 2,3; *Crazy Horse,* 10, 14, and "The Woman Who Rode"; *The Denver Quarterly,* Section 11; *The Kenyon Review,* "Robe"; *Ploughshares,* "Uniforms"; *Poetry East,* Section 6, "My question has always been"; *TriQuarterly,* Section 1.

I would like to thank Julie Agoos, Christianne Balk, Susan Bergman, and Donald Revell for their criticism and encouragement.

For Rabbi Sidney Strome and Irving Howe

Oh! Rabbi, rabbi, fend my soul for me

And true savant of this dark nature be.

WALLACE STEVENS

Rider

I

Got a letter yesterday from a synagogue on the East Side asking
for money to keep my father's name alive. I
balked. And would
explain (not justify). Wanted to walk into the synagogue across

the street for a few minutes just to get a taste. Needed
tickets. Father always had tickets for high holy days too
(never set foot in a temple on any other day). What

am I getting at? I lived
with a Rabbi between the ages of six and fifteen, he was
my mother's husband. We were very tight.

So you never had to buy a ticket because you were the Rabbi's stepson?

No. First, we never used that word "step." Second—and this is what I was getting at—there were no tickets.

Yes, it was assumed that temple members paid dues but anyone who could not afford these dues was still welcome, heartily, not half-heartedly welcome.

Hey, you lived in a lot of places, are you sure?

I'm sure. It's the kind of thing one remembers.

There are a lot of advantages to living in the boonies.

I look at it another way. The right to pray.

I don't think you're talking about tickets. You didn't really want to go. A friend offered you tickets and you hesitated . . .

And finally said no.

I had to think about "the little Rabbi" and I didn't want to do it in the presence of another Rabbi.

I didn't call him the "little Rabbi" when I was a little boy. It wasn't that he was so short (5′9″ on stilts) but that he was frail. My mother and I used to elbow each other when he went to lift the Torah out of the Ark: he must have had help from God.

A Mormon friend in Salt Lake City called him The Brain. First, (he broke down his arguments point by point, often, in later years, by pressing his right thumb against the fingertips on his left hand—a habit that drove me mad) because he was the smartest man he'd come across. (By "smartest" I think my friend meant he used words that hadn't migrated to those latitudes—that valley Brigham Young—standing up in his stirrups—called "the place.")

Second, because he had this enormous head, and forehead, and nose, which dwarfed his body, his stick-thin arms and legs. He was the most bodiless creature I've ever known.

That may have helped keep him alive for over five years after he had his stomach removed.

I think his body discovered heretofore unknown nutrients in bourbon.

I can't separate his charm—what was enchanting about him—from his size. And the hugeness of his forehead, the jut of his nose, his jug ears.

He never imposed God on me. I was expected to go to temple most of the time but—I who could not stomach school—liked it. He was on such intimate terms with God, had thought so deeply about scripture, made the stories so compelling. . . . And he looked so holy in his robes.

This immense head suspended over the pulpit.

(The anonymous Caxinua poem of the moon's creation: "You going to the sky, head?")

There's more. The small communities we lived in in those first years together were welcoming. It meant something more to be a Jew in small towns in Illinois (in Chicago Heights and Kankakee) where there were, at best, a few hundred out of . . . 20,000. . . .

Mourning for him has been difficult. Mourning for my real father took so much out of me. . . . (That phrase always makes *me* bristle.) And then the type of cancer he had, combined with his frailty, made me think of him, in those last few years, in an almost post-mortem way. Every meeting had that feel of "the last" meeting and it began to get to me.

Can you be more specific?

It began to get to me.

I wanted him to live or die, not hover between two worlds—as if this hovering weren't our condition.

And he asked so many questions. He trafficked in confidences.

♣

This is not the time for me to tell you what happened to him in
his worldly life in later years. This is not

a portrait of my torment and ambivalence about
the man apart from being

great to me in many ways when I
was a little boy

(I came to question too much: seeing him (as an adult) lavish attention on young children I began to wonder just how specific his love for me was—or his love for my son—whom he loved—but so did he "love" another two-year-old in his apartment complex in his last place of residence, Florence, South Carolina. He talked and talked about the affection this blond/blue eyed baby showed him, the hugs, kisses. . . . He was nuts about children the way some men are about women.)

And your son, Samuel—can I call him Sam?—isn't exactly cuddle-crazy.

He doesn't cotton-up. He likes to announce how he hates hugs and kisses with an indescribable relish.

You're grateful?

Grateful implies I owed him something.

No, we shared something. We were pals, co-conspirators.

He loved children and as a child I loved him.
Tucked him into bed.
Felt responsible
he was so little.

♣

But by the time I was a teenager the drinking had taken him over so that it was as if he no longer cared. He "quit" the Rabbinate again.

♣

What was a Rabbi's salary in the mid-fifties to the mid-sixties?

Thanks for asking. It hovered around the $10,000 mark.

That magic figure cropped up even when he left the Rabbinate and went to work for General Klein and City of Hope: he was offered $10,000 + 10% of whatever money he raised for City of Hope.

Even numbers. Keep it simple.

But what made that salary so galling was that his average congregant earned at least twice that, and many three, four, five, twenty times more. And then put that 10% of zero—since he was constitutionally incapable of asking anyone for money, "closing a deal," as they put it in the business—against what the actors made who funded City of Hope.

I won't do that. But I get your point.

It was a different world than the world of his childhood.

He tried to marry out of it in marrying your mother.

And look what he got into there: sturm und drang and no reward. Once again he misread the signs. He mistook the fancy address and the accumulated possessions of fifty years for money in the bank he would one day—have access to.

Are you implying something smarmy here?

No, but others have, especially, or should I say predictably, my father.

He called your grandfather a mountebank.

I liked that. But they didn't have to joust and quarrel so much.

I was intoxicated by the Biblical stories he told me as a child; not me really—religion only entered our house on the sabbath—our class at Sunday school. I loved to hear how the Jews overcame obstacles and suffering through miracles and prayer. He spoke "off the cuff," without condescension—as if he knew that children were his deepest allies in this life.

But even when he worked for General Klein in Public Relations he kept his hand in the Rabbinate. Didn't you go to Oshkosh on the weekends?

He went to preach, and pick up a few extra bucks.

Driving through Madison, he pointed out the green lawns of the university. The temperature hovered around zero. A thin aura of ice smote the glass, the grass. A few scraggly downcast students toted book-bags across the Common.

We stayed at someone's house, a calm Wisconsin couple. They had a son (daughters too, but I only saw them running up and down the stairs). We were assigned to each other and we went through the motions of playing Monopoly and Clue. Saturday afternoons we were dropped off at a movie theater where we watched terrible B westerns in a black and white like the five o'clock shadows of Steve McNally and Rory Calhoun.

No dialogue, just shouts and imprecations. All the heroes seemed to do was mount and dismount. No palominos or pinto ponies, just interchangeable bays. Ambush, dry gulch, bushwack—each held at the same passage between the rocks.

In Oshkosh I first felt boredom as a weight. I longed for that sweet shiver of solitude in my basement pup tent, the sheer rustle of absence, of the distance shimmering and fading, not the blank slate of the town in the too bright afternoon sun. The sun, a subtle, serpentine irony in the flux, just heightened the glare off the ice. Our hosts, silvery, benign, reined-in, kept gestures to a minimum. There were no febrile histrionics. The shag rug had tendrils that grasped the cold. I knew I could never explode in Oshkosh. They wouldn't understand. They'd think something was wrong. But this is what really happened in Oshkosh: I sensed clues and signs, keys to the mystery, scattered everywhere, each one radiant and strange, yet by itself impoverished. In Oshkosh I felt my brain begin to curl around an idea, to comprehend the seizure.

♣

But you never observe holidays.

One December I was startled, like some space creature, to look up and see the bodies in the window huddled around the menorahs, the quiet moment ripped out of time, the blind avenue become human for a moment, out of a time yet in time; only one candle lit the first night, the other branches of the menorah scarcely visible if visible at all behind these gray windows in the winter dusk; the story no more than an image of persistence against the odds; the miraculous oil burning beyond its energy quotient. . . .

So oil was an issue even then?

That's what the little Rabbi offered in his sermons:
contemporary takes on ancient themes.

Let's go back. You were walking in the winter dusk. You looked up and felt alone: those others still had rituals, like a balm.

To speak of balm is to speak of wounds. These followers of Mammon claim the right to pray; to be heard by a higher order.

You with your "days of the spirit" have no hope that anyone might hear.

But that's another matter. I was talking about lights in windows at nightfall, at that precise moment when something in your brain clicks and knows it's dark (when it wasn't a moment ago), and the bodies outlined. It is an image of what cannot be possessed, what can never be taken for granted, or taken at all.

⚘

You were a child and
children were his allies.

With his congregants, he played cards.

I don't think he ever lost a hand at rummy.

Now you're exaggerating.

Yeah. But he always always always always
won,
because "the brain" remembered every card that
flashed by.
And yet there wasn't a trace
of competitiveness in his prowess. Things came
so easily to him, a Rabbi at twenty, utterly
bored with what had been his vocation
at forty, ready
to do anything, go
into Public Relations,
work for the corrupt General
("what, a Jewish
General"?) Klein, who cashed in his "successful military career"
for a Public Relations firm in Chicago
"we specialize in
trust" (Klein, later tied
to the doomed Kerner administration, was not known
to be a grafter when Sidney took the job).

⚘

I remember my visits to General Klein's office: the grayness and funereal air and squeaky wooden desk chairs; the embossed citations, plaques on the walls, the golden awards. Though in awe of the General's regalia, I was also suspicious about the nature of "Public Relations." It sounded specious, intangible, unnecessary, a cloak of busyness to escape real work.

A Jewish General! I imagined him in a tank in the desert but somehow his pudgy face didn't fit the image. And yet Julius Klein, being a General, was up there with Hank Greenberg in the pantheon of Jewish *Ubermenschen.* I also didn't understand how Sidney could trade what seemed to me his congenial and social job for this lonely, isolated office with its impressively antlered hat rack and daunting phones. There was such an intimidating air of importance in these offices—yet what were they doing that was necessary for the public good? I was very proud of Sidney around the bigwigs: this was man's work.

I couldn't put the two together, a General and Public Relations. True, even the Korean war had receded, but how could a general consign himself to a desk for life?

I was granted an audience with General Klein around the time of my birthday. He had a drawerful of glossy photos. He pulled one out and signed it. I put on my "awe" face for Sidney's sake, and peeped—"Thanks *General* Klein" unable to short circuit the emphasis on his title. "Thanks," Sidney echoed nasally, and ushered me out.

"What would you like to do now?"

"Buy some soldiers."

❧

We entered the toy department at Marshall Fields: there I saw a thousand antidotes to loneliness, a way to get through endless solitary hours no matter what else happened. Sidney was big-hearted in many ways. He could be generous with time. He could be warm, which is why children crawled all over him at Sunday School, pulling off his glasses (how could he have sacrified *that* for *this?*). But money made him crazy, penny pinching in ways that were convenient to him. Cigars and liquor were necessities. Anything I *desired* was worthy of serious interrogation. *Why do you want it, what for, do you need it, why does it have to be this brand and not that one?* Maybe he thought that as a *step*-father he should go only so far. But the $40 a week my father sent as child-support should have gone a long way to maintaining a child in the late fifties.

He didn't like the idea of soldiers, but after the visit to General Klein's I had him over a barrel. *I would have soldiers then.* Of course I already had a million generic soldiers, whose likeness I saw right away in the toy section—green men massed together, piled in bins—you could get a hundred for $.99. "Here," he said, taking advantage of the opportunity to be done with this expedition as soon as possible, "soldiers. A hundred. That'll keep you busy." I flushed. "No," I said, "I want *these.*" I grabbed a box with a see-through cellophane window from an adjacent table: these men were silver; they had definition; they were three times the size of the generic men; there was one of each type (officer, bazooka wielder, belly-crawling rifleman); they wouldn't fall down when a train went past in the railroad yard below my window. "Why should I buy twelve soldiers for $3.98 instead of one hundred soldiers for $.99?" He had the bag and made a gesture to leave. I broke down. It was my birthday. I wanted a present, a testimony of his love for me. (*What, another test? Another test? Don't you ever tire . . . ?*) I could not get through to him; I couldn't even get his attention. This was torture for him. He looked overheated too in his Fedora and heavy tweed overcoat and cranberry cashmere scarf. "I am not going to spend *three dollars and ninety eight cents* on twelve soldiers and that's final. Have these or nothing." Exact amounts of money, dollars and cents, were given the same vocal emphasis as the names of his favorite prophets when he stood on the pulpit. Venom coursed through me: if I'd been a snake I would have hissed. The simplest litany imaginable was running through my head: "I just want you to buy this for me because it's what I want and it's my birthday."

I could hear it coming: the lecture about the Rockefeller children's small allowances.

They worked so hard not to spoil me.

But he did take you to Marshall Fields and not some cut-rate—

He and my mother had an almost religious belief in the power of brand names.

I concede that one.—And one of your worst moments with them was when you met for dinner near the airport when they were coming back from a tour of Scandanavia, when Sidney, working hard to convince you how wonderful their trip was, listed every country and major city they visited, a string of nouns unaccompanied by the slightest change of inflection.

He just droned on. Pressing thumb-finger of right hand to each successive finger of left hand to mark each passing country with its name.

Can you go a little deeper here?

All right. I sensed that he was in a rage—no trace of calmness; no love in his voice any more . . . as if going through the motions of having had a good time (—he'd paid for it—) had thrown an abyss at his feet which he could neither look at nor ignore.

There was something formless about his suffering—this man who in his first alert hour after he had his stomach removed announced that if he "had to do it again" he wouldn't be "a Rabbi in a thousand years."

Is there ever an end to mourning work?

Only the morning light assuages it.

❧

What are you doing now?

Sitting at a white iron table at Cafe 112
on 112th St and Broadway at 9:15 (a.m.),

the green letters and intersecting
circles of a billboard on a wall above a garage
on the east side of 113th St

simply
KOOL

it says

and the G and the A and the
R are effaced so that the garage sign reads

A
G
E

and the P on the PARK sign is blotted
out by a tree so it reads

A
R
K

D. H. Lawrence in the TLS anticipates my next thought: "The things one cares about are all invisible, like seeds in the ground in winter. But one has to attend to the things one only half cares about. And so life passes away."

An attractive nun takes a seat on another white chair: the threat of her chastity arouses me.

♣

I didn't mind being called Mark "Strome" in the temple world. It gave me a chance to slip out of my identity, and relax, and unshoulder some of the burdens that attached to being "Rudman"'s son (ping-pong ball in the endlessly vicious divorce and custody case). I never cared what his motives might have been for wanting me to be known

in the temple world

as his real

son—

it was simpler that way

all agreed.

—I remember the shiver of pleasure I felt once when Norman Landsman (a boy my own age whose mother was Salt Lake City's greatest Jewish intellectual and high up on the temple board) called me *Strome* in a fit of pique.

Warmth suffused me. He'd missed—his *pique had nothing to do with me.* He was one of the few

Jews I saw
out of temple
in the real
world where I was known (and branded)
as Rudman,
and he still called me
Strome. The non-
Jews around us would sometimes ask—
who's THAT —

("When one is set apart one grows
comfortable with multiple
identities.") at ease
with contraries, the heat

now, in mid-September, more
murderous than any heat
that struck—this—midsummer,
(the heat
of June worse than any heat July or August
offered too) —

2

The weather's the best gauge of chaos.
By morning heat's gone, the threat—

the thread—of thunderstorms
gone: this is what the suicide relinquishes—

the chance that the next day
will be better in some way,

and the emotional weather
clearer too, "the business of living"

less onerous as the radiance takes over
Straus Park and the white-blond hair of two-year-old

Rachel Fishman: gorgeousness
doesn't hinge on age.

☙

Crossing construction planks over gutters
I fend for half-an-hour's quiet and a seat

with a lamp at the Hungarian Pastry Shop,
light flooding these peripheries, layering

the leaves, rifling
St. John the Divine's skyward scaffolding.

And mix this up with a small
prayer for one who is forever

seated alone here at a white iron table,
facing the cathedral

black binder (thick) open to the poems
of "the second book"—(the neat typing,

clean copy, made them already look
inscribed in heaven)—it was a clear

cold morning like this one
"the action of a busy street,"

people reading musical scores, Latin
primers, the radios quacking, then as now,

about the orchestration of troops
to be deployed.

☙

You're quite a cathedral gazer for a Jew.

I like the play of light in the vaults. The arrangement, mass and density of the stones.

Remember the dead
                    but don't neglect
to walk the city
                    these fine fall mornings
it's not like
          there's any chance they'll last
and no guarantee
               they'll come again
or that you will
               be here when they do.

Only the undesired is guaranteed to happen again.
People's beepers go off
                    at the wrong time now;
imagine being on call all the time—even deep
in the woods—shock to the spider
who, with a horseshoe on its back, guards
the curvaceous waterfall, the rock pool,
which fills and empties

while in the night's weird copper-gray light

we lie on quilts in the grass, our eyes trained on Perseus.
Constellations like routes on Metro maps.
A meteor tadpoles past.

Everything is as near as it is far.

I could hurl my shoulder at the door of our galaxy.

It is the unnamed patterns ask to be traced.

♣

(—Is it that we
get so high
on commerce these days, on, not
"the business of living" but the life
of work which is why migraines thrive
when the pressure goes down

and . . .)

"*Goofy takes Junior to the beach.*"

♣

Summer's gone.

It's fall in the garden, too. Temptation's everywhere.
I saw a man pass beneath some scaffolding on Broadway
with a snake coiled around his neck like a necklace—
only the boa's reared head and hissing tongue
were at odds with the tail—which curled
awkwardly around its neckless neck.

The snake who introduced subtle untruth
released us into fall
when he told her she wouldn't
die if she just
took a bite—which she didn't—not then.

The apples which my son needs and loves
as much as Balzac or Cézanne,
to eat and crunch
into my ears before he lets himself be
cajoled into sleep,
drifting off finally
after so much resistance
as if sleep
were death or part of dying—why
else resist so fiercely what makes you feel
better in the morning.

♣

Note in the elevator
NO WATER IN THE D APARTMENTS—
the plumbing waiting to capsize
the landlord postponing improvements
until it will all have to be rebuilt,
pipe by pipe

(I hate the thought of another cold winter
in New York without water.)

Before you take a wrong turn here, take a walk. Remember what the painter said, one walk around the block is enough to gather materials for the day's work . . .

Torn phones. Orange brownstones. Signs
I had not noticed before: *El Bravo Hardware.*

The digging goes on in the tar. Jackhammers, construction
workers shoveling. The crane. The cement mixer.

The books laid out on card tables or Indian bedspreads,
Love's Body, Eros and Civilization.

That metaphorical dawn, now taken for love-beads.
The shiny cover of another tattered paperback (Livre

de Poche?) contains *La Condition Humaine:*
It was a moment—like a chink in the fabric of time

when the old codes were shelved.
To become something was a violation.

Often I look out and think my life
would be better with a view of the river.

♣

Images on which we were reared.
Storming beaches. Invading villages.

Naptime in the Phillipines. Vulnerable necks.
The Jap slitting the GI's throat—

May of '68,
May of '69.

"*Humaine*" and "human"
suspect words now.

♣

And now the screech of brakes, the shrieks of children,
Miles Davis' score of *Ascenseur Pour l'Echaufaud*
the night street

NUIT SUR LES CHAMPS-ELYSÉES (take 1)

below my window, action,
the secret destinations in the lives of strangers,
their scripts written,

ASSASSINAT (take 1)

Jeanne Moreau's deadpan as,

to the trumpet's pulse, she goes up
in the elevator to the snare drum's

ASCENSEUR

brush, its light percussion,
and leather-jacketed hep cats take a last drag,
flick cigarettes, and dart.

♣

The underground video team wouldn't film my script
of pickaxes hammering indefinitely at a wall.

"No more metaphors, man. We're not into fiction, man.
We want what's happening now, in the streets, man, like the rally,
man."

♣

The snow whirled upward that winter afternoon in Patterson
and while I read *Reading Capital*

a battle took place in the musty ramparts of the 200 year old house:
a spider sucked the life out of a fly that was three times its size.

Althusser refused to take sides in May of '68 at the barricades.
No one knows why. Fifteen years later he strangled his wife.

No one knows why. But everyone knows nothing is the same
afterwards for "survivors of the camps."

And during that first cold June in Paris I shuddered
to read that a certain New Wave director's films would be

"closer to art if there weren't always a murder"
but I didn't, then, know why.

3

The heat wave and the high
        holy days have gone the way
of dates marked on the calendar
        that break time up into bite-sized portions.

An empty calendar seems ideal.
        The tension between the ideal and the real.

Between women and men. Parents
        and children. The murderous mayhem.

The women I see on every street say
My husband's never home,
I'm alone with the children.
It's a terrible life.

Or, *it's a terrible life, my husband's*
        home and I still feel like
a single parent with two children.

♣

(The noise outside my window has come
too near, repairmen on the creaking
scaffold, gutteral jabbering,
whine of electric saw, ping
of ball peen and brusque
sound of snow yanked off the air
conditioner; diasporian
white particles breaking up
as they scatter and land on West End
where parents walk their kids to the bus,
briefcase in one hand,
child's warm palm in the other.

The oilcloth covered scaffold
dangles and swings
over the parapets

they are trying to
repair.)

♣

Sitting across from one another
on our yukky sofa—probably the last
time he set foot in this apartment—
he told me he was the first
Jewish chaplain in the Pacific Theater.
He'd told me before but not
with that emphasis, that word order.

♣

An air of finality brooded over that final conversation between you and him in the city when he had flown in "to bless the baby." He said he couldn't imagine you living there with that view of "West End Avenue" forever. "In Chicago you had the whole trainyard out your window, and in Salt Lake your eyes could graze the snow-capped mountains year-round, and in Colorado Springs—you remember what my terrace faced there—." How tawdry the avenue looked at that instant through his eyes! You began to wonder if you'd got everything wrong. But you replied that there was still the chance the moment you walked out the door that something splendid might occur. He mulled over those last words. Half-aloud. Half in prayer. . . . Riding English in Central Park she

Bolts out of the tunnel—
her expression crossed
between danger and delight, her black
hat, habit, and jodhpurs
stark against the muted gray-white of the bay
stallion plunging down the horse path;
the trees along the reservoir
crouched and whispering
amidst the wind-blown cinders and leaf-particles—
even if we were planted here together
we can still converse;
the sun gone off behind the stacks of cirrus,
and winds converging, churning up

the placid surface, the small waves,
like hands steepled in prayer,
racing across this concrete basin
as if there were a way out or beyond
these toy versions of the swells
that off the Maine coast lob an outboard
back and forth; where sailors, in the instant
before they go under
glimpse the mundane horror of a wave
rearing like a clogged filter . . . ;
but even now, as fold on fold of cloud
dims the metallic prisms
of the chain-link fence I lean against,
the bay surges through again, his neck
stretched further out than before,
as she lets go of the reins and leans far—
far forward to grip his mane.

He liked that. But his death still left you perplexed as to . . .

Why have I come to this hall
        filled with encyclopedias
and dictionaries of the dead
        when outside small white birds,
not gulls, not terns, huddle in the sky,
        flying close together while
                they beat their wings,

branches thrash in the wind
        and bent boughs are stark
as shadows on a wall behind them,
        stark and wild and blind,

and kids are selling T-shirts
        with this institution's name,
and for a moment, it is not
        New York but a cordoned off

garden with stone and brick
        to take me back
                                        and gold paint
peeling off the ceilings. . . .

4

But you had the sense that he was always competing with your father for your affection.

Not only my father. He didn't understand my need to develop ties in these new worlds. He tried to legislate over my feelings. He was subject to extraordinarily inappropriate fits of jealousy.

How are you the judge of that?

Many small incidents.

Such as . . .

♣

The boy's name was Warren. He was an orphan.
As we pulled into the weed lot of the camp
in the uncertain March air and patented silence,
I could see him peeking down at us
from a second story dormer window,
like someone who had been dreaming of escape
from the run-down resort: torn up turf; dirt
basketball court, net hanging for its life by one
thin strand of rope; horseshoes, shuffle board;
musty, mildewed cabins with wet bedding;
the stars pressing too hard against our faces
in the catastrophic silence of the nights. . . .
I'd never been left so happily alone,
alone, that is, in Warren's wonderful company.
His talk mimicked the cadence of the stones he kicked.
Warren showed me the mica glow in the arrowheads
and quartz-tipped spears he'd unearthed.
Warren's cigar box overflowed with other people's
souvenirs, miniature monuments, key chains, lighters,
and initialed items like cuff links and bracelets.
He scoured the corners of the rooms of the departed
while his "mother," slip of the tongue there, vacuumed.
"People always leave something behind," he said.

I knew what he meant: taking their clothes
on and off so many times something
had to go. I wanted an initial bracelet
even with someone else's initials.
The kids at summer camp in the Poconos all had
initialed bracelets, except for me,
but who among them had been west
of the Mississippi?
Warren wanted a home. I didn't know what I wanted.
I asked to bring Warren home and give him a home.
"That's ridiculous, he has a home here.
Besides, you only just met."
My mother lamented his stick-thin, soot-blackened frame,
the smell he gave off and his yellow teeth,
his urchin eating with his hands,
his short and choppy hair,
his blousy shirt and baggy fatigues
that gave him a bulk, a volume,
he didn't otherwise possess.
What about his fits of giddy delight?
As the days passed I forgot myself.
I became more and more like Warren.
I would brook no insults about my brother.
It would no longer be me, but me and Warren.
I'd share my meals with Warren, and my desk at school.
Warren could stay and I would just—slip away.
Next to Warren, I felt like I was on a clipper ship
lifted out of the water by the powerful wind-breath
of my two distant coastal families; my warring
mother and "blood" father, her lovely
companionable family in Los Angeles and Manhattan;
his friendly, compliant relations in Manhattan and Bensonhurst. . . .
I dreamt both families were jammed on the deck
of the ship, waving, gesticulating, shouting,
and that I clung to a raft's rope as a great
wave flung me back and back, but the truth
was I wasn't sure I wanted to be near.
I wanted to fly apart—in the nowhere—.
When our two-door Chrysler Windsor
edged off the gravel onto the highway

I thrust my head right where the plush fabric
of the front seat parted like the Red Sea,
and said to my new dad. "You know what.
I love Warren more than I love you."
"You don't know what you're saying," he snapped.
"He's just a little *putz,* and I can get
rid of him with a snap
of my fingers. Presto. See. Now—where is he?"
The seat beside me was empty. I was empty.
And my heart pounded in wild longing for its fullness lost.
I should have kept my mouth shut
but I thought my heart would burst
with that secret locked in it: why doesn't he
understand? It wasn't that I loved him less than I had
but that I loved Warren more. He had the same reaction
several years later, in Chicago, when I announced
my love for Carol, a round-faced, soft spoken blond girl
I'd brought home to play with my electric trains and drink
hot chocolate one brutal winter afternoon. I loved her and
I kissed her in the elevator on the way up.
I wanted him to say: *I'm so happy for you,*
let's put on some 45's and dance.
He said, "You don't know what love is."
And for the first time slapped me in the face.
I wrote my "blood" father of my love and he wrote back
he was glad I was "making *friends* out there."
Why didn't these men understand, I know what words mean,
by love I meant love, however transitory.
One word, two fathers, two red stone faces,
unblinking, dismayed.

5

What about that girl in first grade? The one who hopped up on her desk
when you walked in the room and exclaimed, "Oh goody, a boy!"

You preferred to play with girls
only you didn't know it then.

One of the girls and a seducer of girls.

Between jump rope and guns I chose guns.

Now I see the low desks and windows
and the radiators lined up along the sills—

You are torn at every moment in time, aren't you?

Nearly.

When will you rest?

♣

You did or didn't play with her?

No. Instead I entered a macho battle
with a boy named Otto Blank. He was the
soi disant leader of the pack and would not
let me play "Wyatt Earp" unless I paid
him a nickel, so I made this wager
with myself that I would swallow my pride
this once to get the hazing over with.

But the next day, when he wanted more, you flew at his throat—

and each day, in the half-hour or so after school
in which we waited for
someone to retrieve us,
we fought, Otto and I—

and he nearly always pinned you down.

But he was two years older, a leap-year birth,
and how well I remembered his second, i.e.,
eighth birthday—

you had to say it—Otto is two!

The class cracked up. He started after me—

And the teacher yelled—

Otto! Sit down right now!

The class tittered.

Only ten years after the war and the Germans and the Jews were at it again.

Huh?

You don't think Otto knew your stepfather was the local Rabbi? You don't think he heard anything *at home to provoke his . . . animosity.*

No, I don't.

That's why you're you.

But our quarrel started in the first recess after I arrived.

You arrived in spring. The first grade class had been together all year. And you, confess, wanted to be Wyatt.

What happened to the struggle for racial supremacy?

He identified you as a Jew, walking in the door and wanting to take over, to improve the playing conditions at recess.

I thought the role of Wyatt should rotate.

Uh huh.

A little candor here wouldn't hurt; I can see what you're insinuating: out with it! No, don't impeach yourself with the question.

What, you think I don't know that if anyone in the world could have known that Wyatt Earp was Jewish that Sidney would have known? Or how quickly this sort of discovery moves through Rabbinical circuits? The sermons you could milk out of the material . . . ?

Imagine America switching on its television sets in light of the idea that Wyatt Earp—whose cover as a *noirish* hero in expressionist westerns was now blown open by this weekly program "with Hugh O'Brien in the role of Wyatt"—had been a Jew in "real life" . . . .

So—another experience undergone in the dark of ignorance. Human ways mystify me. I can see no bottom. If things are the way they are because they are that way, I am driven to embrace chance: as an antidote—at the very least a palliative—against unreason. If things are the way they are for no reason than because they are that way, then nothing is determined. . . .

And the first time I got the best of Otto,
 the very second I had him pinned,
my mother (how did she get there, she didn't drive?)
 arrived at the playground and said,
"Come on, dear, we have to go,"
 and I YELLED —

"in a minute, Mom, I've got Otto
 PINNED—"
 and she—
"No— NOW — "

She didn't know what you'd been going through?

She was unaware, to be frank,
 of the darkness in my soul,
 of the heaviness of the burden I carried,

and carried,
 with no clue as to why—
unaware of the inner resistance I had to overcome
 to be among others
 and not break down,
of the effort it cost me to live—a day—

No, the woman whose daily fare
is a wish she'd never been born?

Well . . . she's more stoical and more
easily distracted by the idea
that baubles heal; she successfully transferred

her anguish onto objects and their absence—

The jury is out on that one.

6

What is this about losing respect?

Do I have to talk about it?
He said he feared what I might
write about him when he was gone,
and I told him not to worry.

He worried about the "streak of morbidity" in your work.

He was a man of God, not of imagination.

And it wasn't his fault if he got the shakes.
It was a familial tremor, not nerves.

And it first happened at a gravesite.

Near where Brigham Young did his number—"this is the place."

He called him Friggin Young.

Well, during his bleak tenure in Greenville,
his congregants would tell nigger jokes
and he would force a smile—afraid now to rock the boat—
a mere exercise in stretching
     the corners of his lips—
a fake grin he would have noted
on another face—false faces being
  one of the things we loved
to laugh about when together we observed
  congregants' idiosyncracies,
their ruses, their guises,

like one temple president, the son
  of the "richest Jew in Salt Lake"
who, seated in the pulpit's other red velvet wing chair,
  would expose the holes in the soles of his shoes
while he batted his eyelashes to
  wake himself up—

(though I owe him one: "Rosencavalier"
didn't turn me in for copying
    the wrong answers from Marty Weinstein
on our "final exam" in Sunday
    school prior to confirmation.

He was ashamed for me,
                    young Rosencavalier.

He could hardly disguise
    the curled lips and downcast eyes
    of his contempt
    for this lawless "Rabbi's son"
    whether or not my name
    was Strome or Rudman,

but where teaching Judaism was concerned
    his plodding methodical
reading to keep up each week
    was a pathetic substitution
for Sidney's well-wrought, impromptu riffs.

                    So there!)

Marty was ashamed of me.
I left town.

As night was falling?

♣

In Utah you can drive at fifteen so by age
fourteen a lot of our talk
was hard core car talk

and somehow the word
Volkswagen came up
after confirmation class

(it was no GTO but you could drive
so far on so little gas . . .)
and Marty's father—a redhead like his son—

made his way up the driveway's ice,
smoke billowing from the exhaust
of whatever sleek black foreign car he drove.

Pulling on his elegant pigskin gloves
he announced he'd "never buy a Kraut   car."
I was   bewildered

(what, hold against a country now
something that happened so long   ago?)
and he held my gaze

and I shivered inside the shiver I felt
from the cold   I thought he would
transmogrify into a southern sheriff

and ask "what kind of   Jew are you   boy"
but he didn't have to say
another word

♣

In other words you were ready to leave town.

I'd had it with Utah.

But you wanted to stay in the west, against your father's wishes?

Yes.

Unequivocally?

Yes. Yes. Yes.

But you did submit to psychiatrists and interviews with the heads of schools during your sojourn in the east that summer?

Yes. I didn't say I wasn't ambivalent and/or confused.

Nothing more, your honor.

♣

This was around the time, was it not, that a certain "Penny," from Los Angeles, a family friend of your grandfather's, came to dinner in Salt Lake City . . .

She was a small woman, slightly hunchbacked, who spoke in a low voice. She was one of my mother's major confidantes. My mother had a great respect for her because she was the buyer for I. Magnin's. When the subject of my father came up, as it always did, Penny, fueled by several Scotches, seemed to retract her head into her chest and when it reemerged she spat out this sentence about Charles: "Why he'd stick his prick into anything!"

I blanched. My features stiffened with rage. Sensual and tormented man that he was, whatever he was, what right did they have to tear him down in front of me! She put her leathered multi-braceleted hand on my hand and said, "It's all right, dahlink." I said, "I've never seen him do anything like that." And they continued. "Well he used to screw the maid," my mother threw in wearily.

How did they know so much about him, this shadow, this spectre?

Everyone knew.

There she was, this tiny hunchback, almost a dwarf—this was how she conceived of loyalty to my mother. In reality, it was another patronizing blow, as if my mother had to hear the worst in order not to feel that the failure of the marriage *might* have been her failure.

And while they sat there tearing him down the phone rang and it was—guess who. Your mother handed the phone over to Sidney who, geared for battle, bourbon happy, quarreled with your father about the precise details as to where you should go when you "left town." They had come to an impasse in the conversation when it seems your father said something like "you can't talk to Charles K. Rudman that way" and Sidney said—because this you overheard—"what does the 'K' stand for"—and your father said—according to Sidney—"cocksucker."

And Sidney howled. He would rag him till the end of his days. "Is this Charles *K.* Rudman?"

I DIDN'T CALL YOU A COCKSUCKER, Sidney said, BUT SINCE YOU SAID IT I HEARD YOU WERE A COCKSUCKER.

I DIDN'T SAY IT!

"I am," your father was rumored to have said, probably (possibly?) not meaning it literally, but more within the vernacular of street language, curse-words meaning "sonofabitch," not someone who literally "sucked cocks."

I think so.

Your heart went out to your poor father at that moment, didn't it? Sidney had a way of miscalculating the effect of these shots on you. You knew your father was writhing in an agony of frustration.

Yes.

But Sidney was running with it, relishing Charles' self-hatred, his masochism which erupted at that moment, out of frustration. . . . And for years he loved to tell the story of how Charles "called himself a cocksucker," always *underscoring the anecdote by absolving himself, by making it clear that it wasn't he who first used the word.*

He really rubbed it in.

Can you forgive him?

♣

Only now that he's dead can I let myself feel
how good we were at leaving each other alone.

You had some tender moments with your real father too.

True.

But the fact is that Rabbi Strome abdicated his responsibility as your stepfather at this point; that is, he catered to your wishes, not to your best interests.

But that's a rational way to look at it.

But are you sure he wasn't willing to send you to that "school" in the desert merely to keep you on his half of the continent, and to delay your eventual (inevitable?) shift toward the east? Are you sure his motives weren't entirely selfish, serving his interests and your mother's in their war with your father?

This is the problem with the legal system: it discounts intuition. I think he knew, beyond all that, that I wanted what was best (and worst!) for me at the time, for whatever reason. I needed space. Open spaces. I had to live.

But you could have done both in the east. Why must you think of life in terms of one thing or the other?

I was saying that he sensed some need in me to be *in that place at that time*—for whatever obscure reason. And that he intuitively followed my intuitions.

Now that's fuzzy and obscure terrain.

It was. It is.

And you had done some time in an Eastern school chosen by your father. That must have made your thoughts of the desert all the more sweet.

My father didn't believe me when I told him what the place was like.

Robe

And now I ransack the drugstore counter
with other hunched shoulder blades—
for remedies: Robitussin for cough—(expectorant);
for cough and cold (expectorant and decongestant);
for cough and cold and body aches
(expectorant and decongestant and acetaminophin);
all NON-NARCOTIC—

I remember my first hour
in that summer school for juvenile
delinquents in the Berkshires.
I had no sooner walked once down the dormitory hallway
when an inmate burst from his room
clutching a crumpled brown paper bag
and collared me: "You going to town?
Can you get me a bottle—of—'Robe'?"
He stood in the luminous squalor with his back
to the light that poured through his window.

In those days you could buy
"Robe" with codeine over the counter
but you had to sign for it and he'd used up
his month's allotment.

When I returned dutifully with his bottle
I could hear, through the closed door,
the sounds of stertorous breathing
as if he were being transformed
into a werewolf; he was leaning over in the dusk
with his head in a paper bag, exhaling,
and howling with every exhale
with nothing but a moonless dusk to goad him on.

It seemed like such a small favor.
It was the last time we spoke all summer;
but it wasn't personal, he only left his room
to obtain "Robe" or airplane glue or beer.

And "Robe" to me meant
that apocryphal pageant in Cinemascope,
that smarmy despot whose cape got in his eyes
each time he ordered heads cut off.

Tonight—*Robocop*—a dead composite,
a cop brought back to life and now,
armored, unable to die;
what remnant of being still
possesses him has sunk
to the commands programmed
into his brain, which still retained,
sadly, the real memory of his own
prolonged traumatic human death
at the hands of the baddest of the bad, bad men.

❦

Sidney resented that the rich Rosencavalier dressed like the Ivy League having a nervous breakdown, and nodded off during his sermons.

And he quibbled with waiters. He tended to pick on the victims of the system, like the ticket taker who makes you wait in line; he mistook, consistently, the symptom for the cause. He blocked out things like—if you don't have money to spend go to a cheaper place. My wife, acting for both of us really, once walked out on him in a restaurant in the primavera era where he was bickering with the waiter about the prices vis a vis the size of the portions. And that's how he always saw her after that—walking out ungratefully on the man who was paying for her meal in this upscale restaurant. He hated it when anyone acted out of the precincts of his will. I mean—he might have said something to the racists and left the waiters alone.

You're getting heated up now. Painful meals are legion in families. Atone.

And then the same man who voted for Stevenson now voted for Reagan. Can you believe that?

Can you?

Stevenson had lost the election in November
and all on account of the holes in his shoes.
Prowling Hyde Park, half-manic from being
out of school on a Tuesday, half in mourning,
I envisioned that ruined man on a worn
throw rug in his spartan living room, holding up
the sole of his shoe to show us the hole—
(by "us" I mean the staff
photographer from the Chicago Tribune). . . .
How could Stevenson have been undone
by something so simple, so basic, so
correctible, why couldn't the people
take him on his own terms, why was someone
who *read books* so threatening, as if a
one-two equation between thought and action
were a devastating universal truth;
so what if one glimpsed his skull
beneath his thinning hair
and almost heard his brain working
beneath the taut flesh.
Ike's hairless head never stirred suspicion.
Ike had a *head,* not a skull.

Maybe the holes in Rosencavalier's shoes reminded him of Stevenson. He felt that Stevenson failed him.

And it got on my nerves when he referred to my favorite writers as great stylists—a "stylist" being an inherently minor figure. He applied "stylist" to Bellow and Mailer and Nabokov, not Tolstoy. (Most hated book, the stuff of several sermons, *Portnoy's Complaint.* He hated that "Jew-hater." And no one hates as well as people who hate to hate.)

And his vehemence against Elvis was unwarranted. But you got him back when he couldn't destroy your 45 of "Heartbreak Hotel." He looked like he would burst while his large soft hands experienced the toughness of vinyl.

Heartbreaking, that slide to high tenor on the phrase "lonely street" and even at seven, in 1956, when the song exploded, I couldn't reach it, or sink to the husky baritone of "never, never come back" as I lay on the floor of my room with my ear to the Victrola's speaker, getting a charge yet unable to penetrate the lyrics, to make out all of the words. I heard, beneath the words, another song, a wild tirade captured in the ululating vowels of the tenor passage, "well I" . . . something . . . "been so long" . . . something . . . to "lonely street" and—big octave drop—"Heartbreak Hotel." I thought it was a real hotel on one of the gritty, dilapidated, ill-lit streets I walked.

But he did bail you out, time and again, as when you were getting mauled every day ("every *day?*") *at Kenwood Elementary. He came to school in his topcoat and fedora—with Rabbi credentials as an overlay of his work with General Klein's (then respectable, possibly prestigious) Public Relations firm. Eddie took one look at him striding through the crowd and put his arm around your shoulder and said, unctuously, "my best—friend—" so you ran and intercepted him on the steps and said—"No don't go in, Eddie won't do it again."*

And he didn't "do it again," that day. . . .

Was this before or after your day with the principal?

My question has always been
what could I have been thinking
en route to the playground

that brilliant fall morning: was the sun
in my eyes, did the light bounce
off the chain-link fence into my eyes

as I neared the gate or was I
lost in reverie long before that?
What could I have been thinking

as I watched the kids scatter
before the bell? Did I see or hear
the ball go through the window, the ball

released by Pogo—who didn't need a pogo stick
to kick out your teeth in midair—and still
walk not run across the playground

brandishing my innocence
on the burning concrete?
Innocence. This was the one

thing the student patrol, hauling me bodily
into the principal's office, never
considered; the one thing the principal

never considered as being within the realm
of possibility during the day-long interrogation.
I was not on the premises when the ball

was thrown; I stood at the fence
watching it crash through the window,
watching Pogo leap, twist, and disappear

from the scene. . . . Lying about misdemeanors
wasn't my style of mischief.
I drew a sharp line between innocence and guilt

where action was concerned, and though I was never
exemplary in any way, I was not
enough of a hoodlum to have denied

something so reparable
as throwing a ball through a classroom window—
unless the scattering glass had caught another child's

eye. And yet the principal, perhaps because I came
from the middle-class, never considered
that I might be innocent and spent the day

trying to get me to confess.
The light scalded the venetian blinds
and heated the room intolerably,

while this hairy hulk, whose 5 o'clock shadow
already heightened the whiteness of his shirt at 9,
turned his tannish jacket—silver lined—inside out;

laid it over the back of his chair
and rolled up his sleeves.
He snarled like a pit bull about to decimate a stick.

He flexed his hands again and again
as if to practice wringing my neck.
He sweated. He shouted. He harangued. He shook

me by the shoulders. Threatened
me with expulsion.
Expulsion! I thought that was reserved

for my classmates, hard-core delinquents,
true sociopaths on the fast track to reform school,
12 and 13 year olds repeating 4th grade

for the 3rd or 4th time.
For the first hour, I cried like a normal child
when wronged, and begged to be let go,

but the more the room heated up,
the more hirsute and sweaty he became,
the more his triceps bulked and his body swelled,

the more I clung to a stony silence, a steely-eyed
glare broken by occasional nervous laughter
which, I quickly discovered, worked

the miracle of getting his goat more than my naive
straightforward requests to be believed.
I wasn't pure. I knew if I ratted on Pogo

I'd be worse than expelled.
"Hairy" scorned my request to use the phone.
He'd "call home all right" when school was over.

To my own surprise, I didn't persist.
With the two of us closeted together in that hotbox he began
to wilt, to sag, to breathe

stertorously. The room lay in shadow now
and I had the sense that, one on one, I could break him.
I began to sense the power

of innocence—a thrill of illicit pleasure
when my cold grin brought the blood to his face so fast
he gasped and for the first time that day I felt

guilty. Not as charged, but guilty.

♣

Let's get away from the matter of your schooling. Remember, he fought so you could go away to school in the desert, go further west than Utah, and not go east as your father desired

once it had been decided I was leaving town. Precious, prurient, Salt Lake.

My downfall began the afternoon
when, instead of caddying, I took on
the immense sea of a lawn
where the distance from the edge
into the wood chips and foliage
was no distance at all and, frankly,
I couldn't control the power mower—
when I got to the edge,

it went off on its own, zigging and zagging.

Every time.

The blades went off on their own.

7

An Interruption

This is the first time I've heard about your obsession with Adlai Stevenson. What I remember—with mortification—is a lunch we had with Sam Shapiro when he was still state senator.

I do too. I announced that I liked Ike. And that the democrats were idiots.

Well you humiliated me good that time.

Why? I was just a kid. Sam laughed.

No, he smiled; he was just being polite; politic.

Starched napkins; pewter silverware; stuffed chairs: mistaken colors. Green wallpaper that couldn't make up its mind. Gruesome oils.

That shows how smart you are.
That place just happens to be a monument.
It was then and it is now.

I don't care.

You don't care. Do you know who designed
the place that you thought was so ugly?

This past May I set out on a pilgrimage back to Illinois but a
bizarre illness and the reverse magnetic fields kept me from
proceeding
south of Chicago.

And your mother said

how do you know?

I eavesdropped.

♣

"There is no reason to go back to Kankakee."
What she meant was: I should have
visited her instead. But she was right:

I didn't need to go back to that particular town
to see the *Chicago Tribune* photo of the three men
smelt fishing on the banks of the Kankakee River.

What could I hope to learn, or to regain
wandering a riverbank I never wandered as a child.
I didn't even remember Kankakee was on a river.

What could I hope to find—that the brick
house on Duane Avenue now had an addition,
or even a subtraction—the removal

of the brutal sunporch where I read my father's
letter which mentioned Uncle Jack's death in a P.S.;
(no more barking out stratagems from the corners

of his mouth as he descended his sunken
living room in ruffled blue terrycloth
in front of his awed wife and brother-in-law,

culling the day by drawing his Minolta from the pocket
of his robe to take a quick snapshot
of his polymathic son torturing

the piano with his hands tied behind his back);
the sunporch my mother transformed into a hothouse
choking with rhododendrons,

which I loathed with all my heart with all my soul with all my
 might;
or that there would be a trace of the poster
for *China Gate* on the wall beside the theater

where my friends and I went to a matinee
on my tenth birthday; or that the glass booth
we entered to hear Dell

Shannon sing "Runaway" was still
in "working order," available
to listeners who had to hear

repeatedly the emphasis in Margo Timmins' phrasing of
"But"s and "oh yeah"s in the song
about the horse out in the country

she gets to see "every second Sunday";
or that the standout goldenrod-colored
Frank Lloyd Wright house, then a restaurant called

"Yesteryear," or "The Yesteryear,"
was now a monument where
people can no longer eat or touch

the slippery grayish-green wallpaper.
I loved and loved this small town—
yet the "Yesteryear"s intrusion of culture

gave off an air of dejection.
Wright was wrong for Kankakee.
The restaurant's rough-textured walls

fronted the bruised rocks
of the mustard-colored river.
My mood was low when I passed it

one grainy November afternoon and felt
fall when dark devoured the yellow
leaves that—just yesterday—

blazed like candles on the branches of the oaks!
I don't have anything against Wright:
the dark mood he inspired may have been

intentional, like the overheated
prose of a Gothic novel.
I found refuge in the vaulted rooms,

shadowy and cool,
he forged in the Arizona heat;
his private, necessary war

against an outside temperature
that hovers—painfully—
around the human norm.

❦

I like that song about the horse. It's wholesome. And do I detect a slight echo of the invocation in the rhythm there? "Thou shalt love the lord thy God . . ."

You bet.

Then something did sink in . . .
And yet you claim—.

"____"

There's something you forgot.

Forgot? Or left out?

Forgot. That "oh yeah" you like—

Yeah.

You don't even know why you like it, but the "Brain" remembers. It's an echo of a song by that sweet-voiced, clean-cut Nelson boy (which I did not attempt to destroy) where there's a memorable "oh yeah" like that—do you remember now or do I have to spell it out for you?

No. "Poor little fool . . . oh yeah . . ."

So who's the "fool" now? You liked that song more than the songs you make so much about.

Yeah. "I knew that I would fall."

Which proves my point: that you've forgotten the good and remembered the bad. The pain.

No. It's the pain that remembers.

I still pray for you. Especially when you go up in an airplane.

I had one of those dreams the other night. There was a blizzard. The world got whiter and whiter as the plane waited on the runway. I was traveling with friends. They didn't seem to mind. I got off.

And yet you claim to have loved that hick town. What was there to "love" about it? (Your mother hated it.)

When I say "the town" I mean my friends. A sense of closeness, intimacy, of being part of a community for the first and last time until much, much later. . . .

That's ridiculous. You were always part of the community wherever we lived.

You only saw the outside.

"_____"

I remember walking home with a girl I'd watched and wanted to approach for several years and now her dark eyes scanned my face in the light and leaves tore loose and the windows in the rows of empty houses on the long suburban street darkened—a precise lingering, undramatic only on the surface, an inward hurtling toward winter; I didn't want the afternoon to end because I knew it could never be repeated; any plan to meet this way would create self-consciousness, stiffness, resistance, even anger at coercion; would breed ragging by friends; and as I walked her to her door and she swiveled around on her stoop—her skirt twirling—I thought everything would be all right if I could stay forever here where the light was failing but still luminous; the shadows bundled on the sidewalk, firmly planted in range of her alert, happy, twiggy walk, her slenderness and small bones that gave no hint of frailty, her serene confidence, the absence of indecision or hysteria in her pauses: her house a mysterious sanctuary of what, in those innocent days, was still called "ordinary life."

❦

Why did you have to embarrass me at the Yesteryear?

I didn't mean to do that, I just wanted attention. I was bored, tired of listening—so I said something that I sensed would make

Shapiro's jaw drop–

I *liked* Sam.

He and his wife were a childless couple.

Why does that phrase make my skin bristle. It's like a—tag.

All right so Mark doesn't like it. All right. So I won't say it again.

You're so thinskinned! He let it pass, why can't you? He still asked you to deliver the inaugural address when he became Lieutenant Governor so the "guilt by association" couldn't have been *that* bad.

❦

Forgive me that bit about Ike. The sum of what I knew about Ike was contained in the image of him in the signed

black and white glossy

that my grandfather had

displayed

on his mantle—but next to Schweitzer mind you. (Laughter.) My liking of Ike was thoughtless; subliminal.

Your grandfather, that—!

Stay off him.

So I'll stay off. But what do you *think about a bigshot who buys a box of five cent cigars and stuffs them into Garcia Vega wrappers; who pours cheap scotch into Chivas bottles; who picks up checks when he takes you to some joint that serves tenderized steaks and Heinz 57 sauce and lets you "do the honors" at the Oak Room at the Plaza.*

("Love is not love which alters . . .")

a guy who lies, who aggrandizes himself

(and who treats his daughter like garbage)

(because that's how he treated your mother)

I wish I had the breath!

You're jealous.

Me? (Guffaws.) *Why you're out of your mind.*

♣

It wasn't Leon who owned the jukeboxes, but Hi Grace.
He was a great guy, why every
couple of months he'd drop me off a case
of Chivas Regal prime scotch or
Jim Beam.

Probably hot.

It wasn't hot.
Hi was a gross, fat man, wobbly
jowled but with a heart
of gold: pure gold.

Each time I dropped a dime
into the jukebox you'd say
"another ten cents for Hi Grace"

(as if in awe of anyone who could
"make a mill" by proxy, reel in
the dough without being there
in person).

♣

I'd done with running away
before I ever heard "Runaway."

Every day after school
we'd segue into the town's one

record store and use up our one free play
on "Runaway," saving our

allowances until we could plunk down
99 cents and take home the 45.

With what stoic patience
the lady let us play it

day after day—squeezed together
in the sound-proof glass booth,

abusing privilege, bending
the rules with each hearing,

waiting for Dell
Shannon's tenor to quaver

as it hit the high note on
wa-wa-wa-wa–wo–o–n-der

where our own
voices would break.

♣

I remember the singer but not the song.
Didn't he . . . ?

Yes.

With a 45 if I'm not mistaken.

So—another one.
And you wonder

why I tried to steer
you clear of that death-

driven—noise. You were
surrounded by death

but you didn't know it.
I saw the dementia in your genes;

you had it on both sides.
No sooner had I married your mother

than her brother blew a hole through his chest,
and your father would have knocked himself off sooner

had he not lucked into the head job
in the company Jack built.

(Now do you see why he reserved
the fact of Jack's death for a "P.S."

under the guise of
underplaying bad news . . . ?)

That sounds like hindsight . . .

It is not. I knew you. I saw you.

♣

I could have burst when your teachers asked
"what is Mark thinking about"
because (—and I'm being candid
now that I'm dead—)

I HAD NO IDEA
but I guaranteed them that your —
distractedness was not
hostile or malicious.

But I could not risk
saying that you didn't carry out
certain commands and instructions
because you didn't hear them:

I sensed that while you were a walking
"emotional catastrophe" that the one
lucky card you'd drawn
was an ability to flee

the present—in order to be
more fully in it.
—Don't forget—you were my student
as well as my son.

♣

Your eyes floating
above the radiator's hiss, out
the window, past the huddled,
squinting fence stakes,

while the cold wind whirled
the autumn leaves around;
your lost, tortured, yet rapturous,
expression—as you were drawn

almost bodily toward the dead
leaves as they rode the wind:
you heard pain in their being torn
from their branches; an all

but inaudible click
like a cane tapping in memory
down nowhere corridors;
like an impression that remains

without the source from which it came:
your gaze trained on that
doomed, disintegrating shape
until the instant when,

no longer suspended ecstatically between
destinations, it stopped
falling—and car after car would pour
over it like murder.

❦

I looked out for you! If it wasn't for me
I don't know what you'd be, or where.

You had your trains. Trains to look at and trains
to play with. You hardly looked up
except to look out. And then those
twins—what were their names?—
that lived down the hall would come over
and there'd be trouble.

(Narrator is dying to say—"That's because when I brought Carol home, or Karen, you got weird"—but refrains.)

❦

Uniforms

The Cohen twins. I wish I could erase them!
The two demons . . . never more demonic

than when on their way to Catholic School in Hyde Park
in their uniforms, the blousy white shirts

and gray slacks and medallioned blazers
they never removed even after school,

and wore even on that fatal—final—afternoon. . . .
Twins. . . . Pure malice when together

saint-like and gentle when alone—.
They cheered up at the sight of me

because it was two against one, four really,
more like *eight,* given the chemistry.

They didn't talk much except to ask to be handed something.
The father, I don't remember. The mother hated my guts:

Long before she caught me on my belly
in the freight elevator discovering an untold,

untoward pleasure—after it had risen to our floor—
a precise point on the glans of my penis which produced

a non-erectile, non-ejaculatory orgasm.
The look on my face must have been zoned out,

and it was from that moment when she stood
before the open elevator, her pale face ashen

below her helmet of fiery red hair
and against the reassuring navy of her dress

that she felt justified in her hatred.
I was an evil force, that had been decided.

She looked like the actress Jesse Royce Landis,
who played the reluctant kidnapper in Hitchcock's fifties'

Technicolor remake of *The Man Who Knew Too Much,*
a creature of misguided compassion.

She had a smart professional air but no profession.
She was radiant, virulent with anger.

The three Cohens burned with a fever to destroy me
as if I stood for the undersoul.

And so her boys *should* attack me gratuitously in my own room,
like an octopus, their four arms and legs

everywhere doubling in the flare-up—
knocking my trains off their tracks,

dumping the cattle out of the cattle cars.
They were not boys who indulged in reveries;

they merely smirked, making fun of the very system they embraced,
as if to say just how far their uniforms were removed

from their true selves, while I was utterly
costumed in camouflage to get me less

battered as I made my way daily through the gauntlet
of switchblades and brass knuckles

on the mean streets of Chicago's South Side:
motorcycle boots and jacket, white tee shirt, jeans.

Real danger I countered and survived, with only a rock
clutched in my fist, but the twins were something else.

Sometimes they followed me around the neighborhood in silence,
sometimes they pounced, and once when I led them—

mistaking the calm of their silence that afternoon for benevolence—
to that sacred ground where the orange boxcar sprawled

on the isolated section of track in the railroad yard,
where a secret source of ecstasy was to squeeze through the door and
look out

at the slatted light stretching ahead like a ladder to the unknown. . . .
The twins immediately scavenged the ground for weapons

and went at me with two disused poles, facelessly, robotically,
as if they were beating dust out of a blanket,

poles that disintegrated even as they brought them down
on my head and ears and body, poles I could not

wrest away because they left splinters like the spines
of a sea urchin in my skin. They acted with such

disinterested cruelty, they were no longer,
to my mind—if they ever were—*children,*

but bullies who wanted to dispose of a mess;
as if I had become an inconvenience.

And the sun burned on the boxcar roofs.
And the pebbles along the rails flared,

and Chicago was on fire in the light.
This was happening now.

8

Dropouts

Mace had the kind of courage you could easily mistake
for brawn. I don't know why I call it courage.

Sure, he stood up to greasers. And didn't visibly fret
on the days when his report card made hard fact

of what was already apparent from his absences.
Yet Mace was gifted with an uninflected quickness, a fine

intelligence of his own despair, a knowledge—
as he gunned the engine of his once white '58 Chevy,

with a four-on-the-floor he'd installed himself,
to climb higher into the hills above the city—

of where nowhere was. . . .
Light shadow cutting brusquely across the canyons—

♣

Like everyone else in our class, Mace was a year
older than me. He had stubble on his chin.

I dragged a razor up and down my cheeks
to inspire fast, early growth.

"Don't shave your jowls," friends warned,
knowing I overdid everything,

"or you'll grow hair there later."
Later was a word I disdained, its insistence

on the future tense, postponement—
life on the back burner.

♣

Mace seemed incapable of worry.
His coolness and insouciance made girls stare.

He was always brushing back the shock of raven-
black hair that fell over his right eyebrow.

The same teacher who sent me lickety split
to the principal's office

would lean over Mace's desk and whisper
warmly, compassionately in his ear.

They would nod together. I could fill in every blank.
"What's the matter Richard?"

"Nothing." "If you're having trouble,"
this is where the whispering grew most intense,

"I want you to feel you can talk to me as a friend.
Your work in class is so good, you have so much ability,
    Richard . . ."

Mace would never protest, never defend himself.
Indignation was a country where he'd never been.

"You may hate me," I thought, praying she would not
double the insult of the absence of her concern

for me with a glance in my direction,
"but deep down Mace and I are the same."

♣

Mace and I were running into the same problem
at the same time. Mathematical

wizards that we were we couldn't solve
advanced algebraic equations in our head;

we were vexed by an added integer.
We had gotten this far without lifting a pencil.

History was being sold to us as a dead language
of fixed events and we wouldn't buy.

What *is* a fact, I wondered, and I could see
the same question wrinkling Mace's brow.

♣

Mace's problems weren't academic. His disgust thrummed
like telephone wires in the wind, even his saturnine

presence was deceptive, like his beat-up Chevy
with its secret store of power concealed under the hood.

Mace too began the year in the front row,
placed there on the strength of pure ability.

He sank slowly, buoyed as I was, by the one
assigned book we read, *Great Expectations.*

Mace attended to his tasks in the classroom.
I dreamt of escape via the window's easy access.

There were unknown roads to be driven, gulleys
to be plumbed; girls: a *world* of lovely distractions.

♣

For all the years I lived in Salt Lake City
I can't remember seeing a single bird.

I felt watched in Salt Lake City ever since
that first day when the old geezer stepped

out of the shadows, on a street vast and empty
and without verticals, to reprimand my *Double-*

mint gum wrapper for lighting in the gutter.
But only around the time of Hitchcock's *The Birds*

did I start to withdraw from sight.
I was keen to see *The Birds* the Wednesday

afternoon it opened and I wanted the other—"good"—"Mark R.,"
the irreproachable blond Mormon angel everyone loved, to join us.

Our growling engine brought his mother to the porch.
The sun glared on her helmet of curlers.

Mark had "homework and chores," she said, he "can't come down."
But he had already descended. And stood framed in the doorway.

I couldn't get accustomed to the light
in the trampled meadows around his house,

the glow of dandelions, thistles, weeds.
Mark's red cheeks reeked of aspiration and I could read

his thoughts: *why couldn't I wait until night?*
Why was I dragging myself down?

Why skip history and rifle assembly?
The movie would wait.

But I would not. I was keen,
and, seeking a purging terror to cleanse

me of my dread, I sat alone with Mace
in the vast empty theater alive to each

click and flicker in the projection room,
and the radiant impalpable dust

caught in the unstinting beam;
released from the limits of our world

until the screeching stopped
and, looked at askance by strangers,

we stepped into an iron dark
which held no trace of the light we'd left.

♣

I forked over whatever change I had
to fuel each day's free-wheeling splendor.

One morning, knowing Mace was down to smoking butts,
I brought a pack of my mother's *Kents*

as an offering. Mace scorned them.
He only smoked *Marlboros.*

Yet later, desperate and broke in the maze
of roads through the hills overlooking the city,

he broke off the filters and smoked in silence.
I was used to doing the talking

for the two of us but this was different.
He pulled up beside a long driveway.

A vaulted roof jutted above columns of tall firs.
This was where he lived. He'd be

"a sec"—he had "some smokes" stashed in a drawer.
I followed him past the plaster jockey and the massy trees

toward an opulent, utterly contemporary house,
fronted by oak door and gold bell-knocker,

angular, white, high-ceilinged, skylit. . . .
Our apartment could have fit into the living room. . . .

Now I understood: Mace lived *in* the clouds.
Though I couldn't see beyond the back yard

through the landscaping I knew what the view
must be like: that was the reason to live there;

for the nights, when the city, innocent as it was,
still blazed through its grid of interlocking lights.

♣

On May Day, Mace and I, long ago tossed
out of R.O.T.C. for "insubordination,"

but required to attend the final show-of-arms
sat together in the bleachers,

in splendid isolation, and watched
as the rule-followers—led

by the many-striped, other Mark R.—
in their woolen khaki uniforms,

shouldering their M 1 rifles,
dropped like flies in the insuperable heat.

9

And when he told you how long it had been since he'd had sex with your mother you felt discomfited, as if you, who disregard so many boundaries, wished he hadn't stepped over that one—wanting to preserve some distance between you and these children who were supposed to be your parents, for whose well-being you were responsible even if you were not "responsible."

It breaks down this way: after I went East he felt hurt and betrayed. I was now in my father's camp.

He "made friends easily" with pawnbrokers and racketeers, people with whom he had nothing in common, beyond the love of baseball, booze, and schmoozing. He was drawn to the dark side. To shadows and money. People with underworld connections.

> Money. I want it I need it I love it.
> To rub my body in lovely greenbacks.

And Chicago Heights, you later heard, was "where all the gangsters lived."

Sidney's best friend there was a man named Leon. One Friday afternoon his son, David, and I stopped by his dry cleaning outlet to cadge some pocket change. There was a man facing him at the register. Black hat, greatcoat open, collar up. Through the seamstress' curtain I could see his fleshy, intent face in the mirror. Leon's palms faced outwards; he'd soaked through his shirt; he mumbled he'd "get it." Then the man was gone. Whatever we wanted that afternoon was wearily offered: soda money, endless slugs to plunk into the juke boxes and pinball machines he'd strung across these splintered suburbs. . . .

❧

You still don't understand how this student of Stefan Wise and Martin Buber could stop caring.

He was never happier than the week he schlepped Theodore Heschel around Salt Lake City, talking about "the hearing of voices," the intimate link between prophecy and psychosis.

♣

We were happy when, alone together, he didn't have to talk. Waiting for my plane in Greenville, we walked on the airstrip, the yellow grass heavy with planes left over from the war, thirty, forty disused planes.

I can't describe the love that flowed between us at such moments.

Why were the planes there, like some fabulous exhibition.

♣

"This is some Rabbi," my grandfather would say, winking and giving the phrase a winsomely ironic twist, more bemused (insofar as it did not effect the rest of our fates directly) than contempuous, the irony a worldly person has when they discover that men of the cloth want what they want too.

My grandfather was dumbstruck that Sidney would argue with him about the Dow Jones ("what does a Rabbi know about the market?") but the last straw was when he had the gall
to order a
steak in the Oak Room,
—"if you wanted steak I would have taken you to Delmonico's"—

That was another meal you never forgot. The five spot crumpled into the waiter's hand.

No, I hated both of them for going at each other. I regret what I did but I was desperate.

A radio blared in the men's room, Ben Gurion's name, again and again. Sat down at the table, folded my napkin over my lap, and announced that Ben Gurion was dead. That got them.

They blanched?

The two of them, absolutely white, dead in their tracks, voiceless.

But you felt like it was overkill.

It was like killing them. But I had no other way of interrupting their quarreling and it was making me sick. My idea of a good time would never be going out to dinner with more than one other person.

You've always been better one on one.

We all are. As a child I felt like an outcast because I did not like groups—group mentality. The pressure of wanting to speak would build up in me and burst in my brain.

Ah, shyness. You're lucky you didn't start stammering.

I almost did. And anxiety's shallow breathing made me feel lightheaded.

♣

Remember the time in Chicago—he liked to remember it—when, on the doctor's recommendation, he dragged out into the blizzard to get you some Coke.

My happiest sickness.

♣

Your last visit took place under auspicious
circumstances. You had gone
to see him under protest, under duress—
not long after the hurricane
leveled the Carolina coast and your mother wrote
that this was "real life" and not "reel life."
—Thank god for step-parents! Got any handy?

I just met a woman who, though in love with a man, said she would die if she had to wipe his two-year-old's ass, and left him.

Sidney wiped yours.

And reminded me of it the rest of my life.

The rest of his *life. Your life is still going on! Were you sickly?*

No. Monday and Thursday to the Rosenbloom brothers, the allergists, for shots, Saturdays to the psychiatrist; didn't miss much school except when I pretended to be sick.

"Never missed a day" from asthma.

Never.

Never?

I could explain. . . .

Feel free.

Asthma . . . is a kind of premature entombment.

Can you be more specific?

It always comes on without warning. Deep, deep in the chest, where nothing can reach it.

Did you take precautions?

Told to avoid dust and molds, trees and grass, animals, rotting leaves, sunflower seeds, and overexertion, I'd come home after hours of football in the dead leaves, red-faced, thick-chested, radiant with dis-ease, proud that I could breathe through the wheezing, through the presence like steel wool, in my lungs, unexpungeable, limitless, forever expanding, like death in the cells, until there'd be no room left—and let my mother administer the tablespoon of dark liquid with the magical name—*Elixophilin*—and wait for the wheezing to subside, which it never did.

How bad was it really?

There was only one unendurable moment and that was to wake at say, 3 AM, gasping, disoriented, as if buried alive in a coffin of air, the world, the earth, perceiving no comfort there, unable to breathe lying down, unable to endure sitting up, calling for my mother who brought back the bottle and the spoon, and stroked my wet head and changed the sweat-soaked sheets. By the time the sun rose in the window my chest would be clear. But all the medicines, instead of soothing, hopped me up: I'd get out of bed light-headed, strung-out, pull on boots and jeans, swallow some *Cheerios,* sit on the stoop and wait for my ride to school and an eight, ten hour reprieve.

I welcomed school as a relief from the torment of those nights.

Each morning I made a private wager with myself that the wheezing would not recur, and each night I lost.

Asthma was a kind of high, a crash course in sensation, a premature secret knowledge of mortality, burying any hope beyond escape from present symptoms.

But you did have—confess!—a higher sickness.

I confess. A dread so deep as to be nameless; sourceless, unexpungeable.

It comes back when the propellers of a turbo-prop start to turn in the fog.

❧

When he ran to his Barca Lounger at the news of his mother's death he removed his glasses and wept. I could not tolerate his suffering and matched him tear for tear. He now spoke of his mother as a paragon, a selfless teacher—a saint.

He put her on an elevator to heaven. . . . But his family played no role in your life.

You begged to meet them but there was "no need."

You walked up the tenement stairs broken and cemented by Yiddishisms, the smell of corn beef and cabbage. His parents waited quietly in their doorway as you approached the threshold. Both his parents were small, but

Sidney hadn't warned me that his mother was a hunchback.

"*Humble*" *was his epithet for her. . . .*

She sat us down at the kitchen table. It took his mother so long to make it from the dining room to the kitchen (how the floor creaked and groaned!) for tea and pound cake that her hump became fixed in my mind as signifying the burden of years and toil.

Because of course you wouldn't have known the difference between her "condition," which accompanied her at birth, and the deformities that are the result of hard labor, like "sitting hunched," which would have made more sense if she had been a seamstress and not a schoolteacher.

No . . . I wouldn't have known. . . .

You didn't understand why Sidney wanted to spend all *of his time in New York hobnobbing with your grandfather (but don't tell me you ever entertained the thought at any age that the Strumphs would have been invited to the House of Levy for the wedding reception) . . . ; why* all *the attention should be paid to your mother's family just because they were glamorous and boasted an address worthy of the* Monopoly *board.*

Strange world!

Is it that she was old and poor and lived in a tenement in the Bronx that made her unworthy, in death, of her son's presence?

His brothers probably covered for him.

He should have gone to his mother's funeral if he loved her as much as he said he did.

Families have unspoken rules.

This old woman who demanded nothing more than a bi-annual phone call (what would she have done with "presents"?) would never have expected her shining son—who began bringing money home at the age of seven by giving Hebrew lessons, who by the time he was eleven held the entire congregation in his thrall with his low, melodious voice, who graduated CUNY at eighteen and was ordained by the time he was twenty—to come to her tawdry grave. *What, fly 2,000 miles east over mountains to see me when I am dead?* Not for her Keith Douglas's refrain: "Remember me when I'm dead."

IO

I was a boy in Kankakee waiting for services to end
so I could take a dive in the leaves
no school for Jews, the whole day
given to imagining feasts
and freedoms, my stepfather
transformed into holiness by his job.

And I will always see him pulling the Torah out of the Ark
and taking off its sky-blue shroud.
He looked so holy in his robes,
a small-boned man in ascension;
a head, suspended over a white cape;
a voice, quietly urging patience:
you will get home to guns and football soon.

Some things it's better not to get over.

I remember how, as he preached, you would scrunch your face,
or imitate some buck-toothed, do-gooder's eager attitude—
and he would raise his eyebrows and gaze down
at you in mock consternation.

—But he didn't quite get what the school meant
by "discipline"
or what the fuss was about
when, in Junior High, you were nabbed
with his Varieties of Sexual Positions *in the playground,*
while your Mormon classmates piled over your shoulders
urging you to turn the page.

He couldn't bring himself to think of these trespasses as sins.

And yet he balked and reddened
when you confessed your prepubescent romance
with the girl in the elevator

and continued to betray my intimate revelations,
repeating them brusquely to guests and strangers. . . .

(By the time I was seventeen this had gone to
"Do you use protection?"
as if I had passed from novice to master overnight.)

It must be difficult for a Rabbi to have to play
father to a juvenile delinquent.

Whenever I was expelled or put on probation he took my side, agreed that the officials were schmucks, but that they couldn't all be schmucks: some of it had to be my fault.

You wanted to please him because he didn't pressure you?

He always took my defense in the community as on that afternoon when I'd stopped in to pick him up at the temple. He was wrinkling his eyebrows while reading my report card when we were interrupted by this lady who just "happened to be passing by" (in a neighborhood ten miles from where we lived) and just wanted him to know what I and some other boys had done to her car in addition to washing it.

What was the nature of the offense?

The denting of her fender upon impact with the glistening hubcaps of another car in the compound.

So you drove the cars to the site where the washing was to take place. The owners assumed you all had licenses.

She claimed I had taken her car under false pretences. Sidney listened to this righteous bitch blow up our error (I was not driving) into a conscious act of vandalism and looked at me "more in sorrow than in anger," and I could feel he was thinking something like:

"I don't know how far to go with this boy. I just hope he works out whatever's eating him."

I could see him registering, beyond the immediate crisis of my report card and the woman's complaint, the chaos in my brain, and praying, in his way, that it would find its way out before it destroyed me.

♣

Tell me if I've got it right: "good" congregations in "nothing" towns, lousy pulpits in meccas, or brief, spectacular turns as a replacement.

His salary being what it was the congregation tried to make up the deficits in perks: discounts—which became his fetish—

so and so gave me Cuban cigars,
so and so bought me a bottle of Chivas Regal,
so and so bought me lunch,
so and so bought me tickets to see hookshooting Billy "The Hill"
 McGill
score sixty points for the Utes in another losing battle.

This roused even my mother to broach the joke he'd walked into: "and so what did *you* buy *them?*"

I would have thought, from his upbeat phrasing, that each of these occasions was a small victory—but over what?

I had no idea then that there was an underside to these announcements: all these "gifts" sounded like extras: not compensation for a deficit.

They disguised his humiliation.

♣

You even learned Hebrew under his tutelage—the only "homework" you ever did— . . .

The way he taught it
I could learn it. That was one A−
I earned.
 (First it was a
B+; the class protested: he was happy
to change it.)

♣

You exaggerate certain aspects. He also had friends who were his peers.

I know. But he saw them on his own,
usually at lunch, or after dinner
at the Officers Club in the Rotunda
with the "best view of the valley"
where he whipped everyone nightly at gin.

(*And sometimes handed you a fiver, perhaps 10% of his winnings, on the nights when he won big—considering the moderate stakes.*

How timidly he confessed these bursts of generosity to my mother in the kitchen come morning, as if wondering whether she'd kiss him or kill him.

Or demand her share.)

I never saw these legends, (none of whom
were Jewish), these wise and worldly men who did more
than survive, who—thrived.

His voice didn't rise the way it did when he was among Leon and other simple souls and could regress to a mean.

Or that old guy with the hearing aid. Happy.

He loved Happy like a father. I preferred his wife but I liked Happy too because he was so happy to see us.

Come on now.

No, you. I was seven years old when I knew these people! They were like an adopted family. Maggie and Margerie (my mother) once visited me in the desert together. And I didn't mean to imply that Happy and Maggie were simple. They weren't. They were sympathetic and had big family troubles of their own, the two unmarried sons, the twin taxidermists, the daughter who married a Lutheran.

I thought Sidney could protect me from anything
because he was
                    pure spirit—never saw him fearful
because he was intimidated by another man's physical strength,

like the time you threw peanut shells down the bleachers at the Salt Lake City Bees game, and an Indian who'd been showing signs of irritation all along stopped craning his neck, stopped squinting, stopped wishing you would stop . . .

It upset me to see Herb Score—unstoppable, unhittable, until a line drive by Yankee Gill MacDougal smacked him dead center in the forehead—get knocked around in the minors. I remembered photos of Score in the hospital with the great gauze bandage and the shattered grin. But hope—broke through: Score would play for the Indians again in Cleveland and I would be airlifted from this horrifying pure and virtuous environment. Where to drop a gum wrapper—

and vaulted toward you, leaping railings, flushed with rage. . . . Sidney waited until the next day to tell you how scared he really was as he worked to ease the man's anger in the hope he wouldn't smash your face.

Hey, I wasn't the only one throwing shells.
Lucky hid behind my mischief.

But you could never get enough.

No, never.

And after the Car Washing Incident Lucky's mother wouldn't even let him come to the phone.

I can't go on. It's so squalid.

Maybe a certain pattern was established early on between you and the Rabbi?

Sidney loved to tell the story of our meeting. The first time he saw me, I was wound up: my grandfather and I had been boxing. I came running into the mirrored room with the chocolate-colored boxing gloves on and when Sidney reached out to shake my hand I gut-punched him—to please my grandfather. I packed quite a punch for a five-year-old. Sidney said he did his best to smile to conceal the pain and claimed he swore to himself on the spot to "crush [my] testicles" in revenge. But Sidney, no "gentleman" by my grandfather's standards, was a gentle human being. His notion of sparring, except for an occasional attempt at spanking, was entirely a jousting of wit.

What errand was he running
that yellow-blue October morning—
your first fall in Illinois—
when you let go of the emergency brake
on Chicago Heights' steep Main Street . . . ?

I hid under the wheel,
my hands cupped over my eyes,
my life in the hands of the stranger
in the red and black hunter's jacket and hat
who pinned the dove gray Chrysler
to a standstill.

He was quiet on the ride home.

It was the moment to broach the question.

"Would you give your life for mine?"

"Yes."

"Can I have a milkshake?"

"Yes."

But when I wanted to eat alone
on our first night together
as a family in the "rent free"
lime green stucco prefab ranch house
to watch an animated *Swan's Lake* . . .
he was enraged.

"You'll eat with us!"
I didn't budge.

Who was this guy giving you orders?

Mother lit the candles.

This was the first time you had your own room.

I had to share it with the unpacked
boxes and crates and bruised
my left rib (good for three days in bed)
on a hard cardboard corner
diving for cover
when my attacker crept silently along the eaves
in mocassins and fringed buckskin.

That sounds better than exploring the basements
of houses of construction with your friend
who locked you in with the poisonous
cotton mouths and water mocassins.

♣

What about his view from the terrace of Pike's Peak?

He talked about that view too damn much—

Sat too many hours alone on that terrace
flicking ashes into the infinite
watching the fireflies and the amber colored
liquid in his glass
mate with the dusk. Too much
alone. In spite of his shrieking
social life—
                    if you'd ever want to call
an itinerant preacher's rounds and duties

social   life

                    There would be
the invitation to the country club,
a game of cards. Talk, cigars.

And the first week we were in a new town
kids would be assigned to me. They were

offering bodily proximity, not friendship. I would
set them straight right off, "he's not my father,
I don't need your charity." And make
friends with the kids in public school
to whom I was just another kid.

In other words the special treatment you desired wasn't of this sort.

You've got it.

Stop trying to trick me.

Ask the right questions.

I didn't tell you not to render the landscape.

No, but then you make me put it in terms of his hours on that porch.

It was like a Chinese scroll really, man contemplating mountain. He was "heavily into" the mountain's changing colors, the purples and golds; whatever was ungreen, unbrown.

Which is why for a long time I could not look at a sunset. —And then there were my father's purple postcards about breath-taking sunsets on the bay.

He began to look like a sunset. And there was nothing left.

The two old codgers mumbling about mountains and waters.

Nature as kitsch.

Cruel boy!

No, I would have preferred rage directed toward the object.

But rage always exceeds its object.

And this was where language stopped: it could not scale Pike's Peak from the terrace.

The world is not something to look at; it is something to be in.

II

And yesterday something shattering happened.
Not yesterday, but several (that's becoming
a favorite word) weeks ago I came across
Kitaj's The Jewish Rider and wept:
there he was in the very image of my stepfather;
the pate where a few strands of hair still frolic,
the same skinny legs, the same misguided
attempt to dress in a sporty way (who's
watching?), the same abstractedness,
the same shlumpy—boneless—posture, gazing not
at the landscape flashing past
with wires lashed to the treetops as if with one
tug the countryside would vanish,
or listening to the tick of the rails,
but fixed—distractedly—on his lower extremities,
white loafers and the crease in his pants and nylon
socks to see whether or not he should roll them up . . . ;
no: looking both beyond and through physical space
into an inner dark. Why else draw the eyes as shadows?
It's his glimpse into another world.

☙

My mother's father hunted and rode.
      My father rode and fished.
My stepfather never budged
      from his Barca Lounger
once the amber liquid began to pour.
      He had a spiritual life
and a social life and no
      physical life. But he liked it
that I was always outside:
      maybe that's why he never
got on my back about grades;
      he might have thought
that *this boy has to be outside*
      at this time in his life.
Maybe it's more important

that he roam the canyons and the hills
that he know the streets
that he come home
covered with leaves and bark and mud,
than that he sit there
like a good young scholar
like I was, a Rabbi
at twenty giving money home
to my parents in their cabbagy tenement
in the Bronx. This is a boy
who needs space. One time—
I think I had my learner's permit—
he rented a Mustang
convertible in L.A. and for several
days I drove around
past the long rows of used car lots
and the bruised facades of restaurants
digging up relatives, my hoarse-voiced
arthritic aunt in the shadows of
her goldenrod colored ranch house,
limping like Ruffian
after her last run
in the wet dirt at Belmont Stakes.

♣

But I've said nothing about what made me weep.

It's in the contrast between Kitaj's alter cocker
seeking comfort on a train,
and Rembrandt's taut youth
setting off into the rampant amber on horseback;
it's in the image of active life juxtaposed
with the image of sedentary contemplation—
though no one travels on horseback now
and heroism has become
attending AIDS patients
or sheltering the homeless.

The raw youth's feet are planted
lightly yet firmly in his stirrups.
His coat glows with many colors.

Not so The Jewish Rider.
And yet—there's something more.

♣

Michael Hoffman writes that New York
is not what it was when I was too young
to have marked the existence of The Blue Note,
but I can pick up this trail
by walking across the park to the Frick.
And Barbara Hershey wouldn't have been at the Frick in 1959
(they don't allow children under sixteen)
in black skin tight pants, black sweater,
(the female uniform of our generation
whose male version substitutes
black jeans, baseball hat, and bomber jacket—
though who knows what decorous garments
she'd checked in the cloakroom),
and white boots with plenty
of Elizabethan ruff at the edges,
pausing to look at The Polish Rider
while I scribbled notes. Her white
boots stood out against the dominant dark
like the Jewish Rider's white loafers.

And that was good because the light in the painting is brief
whatever the time of day, sunrise or sunset,
and the rider's gaze, looking out over
unknown space, is inward.
I followed his eyes through the archway toward canvases
where clouds roll over harbors
against the whiteness of sails
or toward gilded robes and velvet-hung rooms,
then back to meet wisdom's bared breast
in Veronese's Wisdom and Strength. . . .
(Why didn't Veronese have the nerve

to call his painting Woman
With Bare Breasts, like Tintoretto?
Why an allegorical title when the bare
flesh and bones and sinew would have done?)
He spends his life looking not
at far off hills or citadels or
the lights in the village below:
he has no choice but to fix
on her one bared breast, her swelling nipple.
I can't figure out what landscape
he might be facing in the painted world.
The clatter of rocks and hooves
echoes over the stony plain.

⚘

I was no rider, but a pretend
horse and rider always rode
beside my train window—at a canter
no matter how fast the rails clicked by—
and though he wore a bandana
and leaned slightly forward in the saddle
to pull himself aboard,
his gaze, wide-ranging yet intent,
was like the Polish Rider's.

Even as an only child I was never lonely.

My mother's father rode until he was old
and on a narrow pass his horse
jammed him up against rockface.
In his narrative of his life
this collision marked
the ruin of his hip
the rise of his cataracts.

My father rode "every morning before work."

I never witnessed that,
but at a ranch in upper New York State

while I bloodied my hands
tugging the reins of a frothing giant
who would not budge from a weedpatch,
I watched him disappear
in his black polo shirt and khaki jodhpurs
as he galloped over a far off hill:
more at ease in the saddle—in the air—
than I'd ever seen him in civilian life.

My woman friend in El Paso lives to ride.

Only the Jewish Rider and I do not ride!

❦

That's the stuff of events. What about
the signature inscribed by the sun,
the dark clouds sinister in just being there;
thresholds, exchanges going on in the village below,
candles lit in the deep interiors,
bread, wine, the plate making its way
around the table; what about—

leaping centuries ahead—
the energy from generators blazing
like auras through the clouds,
and, looking down from the heights,
the scattered lights,
the rotating tops of ambulances;
the tuna casseroles and macaroni and cheese

making the rounds, apple sauce
passing from high chair to bib, the Wonder Bread
on a calcified plate,
children eating, heads down, in silence,
communicating through eye movements,
the mother wiping her lips, the father
grinning stupidly and drooling;

the television quacking in the background,
the perfect suburban night unfolding
in bedroom and drive-in and den,
the sprinkler system ticking.
The snipers in the tower—.
This is what the riders,
guests everywhere and nowhere,

say goodbye to as their horses break into a canter
as night comes down. And last
night, driving to Connecticut,
I understood that the Polish Rider
gleans the permutations of light after dusk,
that its olive-gray smudges reflect
the absence of pitch-darkness. I was wrong

about the Polish Rider all along:
he doesn't depart at nightfall, he stops for a moment
crossing difficult terrain (anticipating rockslide?)
in the night, because, as the faint light
rimming the edges of the sky makes clear,
night is not absolute black, but rough-hewn and curious.
The rider lives in order to depart.

The Woman Who Rode

She hitched her horse to the gateposts of my house.
Bare trees, frost, the whole bit.

I wanted our lives to be like that:
as rife with silences as a Quaker meeting.

She came to me in her stride.
Dropped her crop on the chair.

Peeled off her britches and boots; crawled
under the covers.

Her hour in the saddle had "made her ready."
I felt like an accessory.

The wound was open. Drowsily I rolled
onto her, no longer caring if she

was using me. As the new
year wore on and black ice made riding

a fast track to certain death
or paralysis, she grew tense.

Came to me now with clinical terms,
"schi" words I worked hard to break down.

The good news was she was not a true
"split personality"—the glitch

that "she was divorced
from herself, and could not love or care."

♣

The light in her house
was like the light before dawn.

On the last of my rare visits
her mother jarred preserves while we watched

instant replays of Robert Kennedy die and die.
Her father skulked upstairs, perhaps

testing gadgets; or wishing me off his daughter;
or taking precautions I would not overhear

what words were ricocheting
on his "hot line" to the patent office.

♣

Any objective observer standing back
from the distraction of the impinging present

could see that her torment overleapt
any visible signs and that she was—

as a WASP "rider"—the wrong
person for the place she was in.

Her resilience could not be in question.
She lived to stray from known paths

to leap stone fences and break into open fields.
When her horse went down in an Irish bog

and she was trampled—hooves branding her cheek—
the next day she up and mounted him again.

♣

When she came to me in the dream last night
her smile had loosened.

How lovely she looked in her blue silk blouse.
How well it lit up the colors of her hair.

12

And guess who is on call when another “rider,”
an earthly “Mr. Angel” blows into town. . . .
(The name has not been changed to protect anyone.)
Sidney said “you might learn something about life”
by seeing where Angel was staying—
a camp on a lake on the outskirts of town.
I didn’t want to drive out to see Angel
but Sidney so rarely made demands of this sort—
so rarely pressed me to do anything more
than *look* at his creaking Everyman
editions of Spinoza’s Ethics or Donne’s Poems
that I couldn’t say no.

Besides, we always enjoyed our outings
together, away from his quarrelsome
patter with my mother.

(*Quarrelsome? they transcended viciousness.*)

When we crossed the tracks we entered another world.

The white houses badly in need of paint.
The tires in the yard. The broken swings.

The midday road spread through the fields.
Bluejays squawked in the blighted elms.

The reeds were withered.
The cabins were a place you’d go if you were on the run.

We knocked on Angel’s door. He opened it. Angel was the first square man I’d met: broad shoulders and hips at the same angle. He had a permanent five o’clock shadow. Angel was hairy but he was no slob. Outside of his suitcase on his cot and a glass of water, hall-full, on the deal table, there was no mess or chaos, no sign of life in the room. “I am Karl An(***nn***)gel.” He spoke and moved with the deliberateness of someone who’d had his body snatched. He wore a suit right out of the forties, which further squared and broadened him. I wasn’t familiar with his form of madness. I knew hysteria raised to a higher power, wild gesticulations and flailing, not this buttoned down, bolted, coiled tightness (though in retrospect I had already witnessed Lucky's father Elmer wandering around in a daze, mowing his lawn day after day, getting down on his hands and knees with scissors to trim the grass on the borders of the hedges and flowerbeds).

Angel had had "some trouble" and hoped to "work a few hours a day" somewhere. The next thing I knew he was invited to dinner. Angel refused a drink—a sure sign something was wrong. (I, whose heart's desire was to order a drink in public, couldn't understand Angel's refusal—but who knew about stun drugs then?)

Angel was an outpatient from nowhere. And as a Jew he had every right to get in touch with the local Rabbi. I eavesdropped as they discussed Angel's possibilities; he could work at Penny's. But doing what? I couldn't imagine Angel as a salesman and, because he was a Jew, I thought it was inappropriate that he should use his muscles carrying heavy merchandise.

(Why couldn't Sidney pawn Angel off on the Orthodox Rabbi, that cross between Bela Lugosi and a penguin, whose goody-two-shoes daughter sat across from me in English class? [The odds against this seating arrangement, given the size of this high school, 2,000 kids—overwhelmingly Mormon—were astronomical.])

My mother prepared a gourmet feast for Angel, her special super juicy pot roast with lots of shallots and carrots; and, holding the silver tray decorously at his side, asked if he would like some juice from the meat and Angel, as if offended or rudely interrupted from reverie, "no—no . . . I do not like . . . the juices." "Perhaps some Worcestershire Sauce," she continued. "Or A1 sauce," Sidney piped in. "No thank you," Angel said.

Several weeks later, Sidney came home and collapsed in his Barca Lounger, visibly shaken. "Mark, I needed you today. Our Mr. Angel went a little wild."

I didn't have to ask to hear the rest of the story.

"He'd come to the office about a personal matter. He was clearly in a state of agitation. He was standing right where that woman had come to complain about your 'driving.' And when I suggested he check himself into the hospital he put his hands around my neck and squeezed."

How did Sidney survive this attack?

"I told him 'you can't kill me, I'm God's agent. I'm the only chance you've got.' 'Got,' Angel muttered as he released me."

"GOT!" Sidney quipped—relieved to be free of that idiot—as he stirred a highball and shook his head at the same time.

"I might have reached for the letter-opener. But I couldn't let him turn me into a killer."

13

Where are you going?

Why?

Why do you have to . . .

Well I want you back no later than. . . . (Studies watch.)

All right, all right.

Don't get impatient. What are you going to drive?

Well, if you aren't going out. . . .

And what if I have to make a house call? (Flips me the keys.)

Do you want me to call you every hour?

Just be back by—let's see it's—eight o'clock now.

It's 7:30.

Well my watch says twenty three minutes to eight. Your watch is slow. Get it checked. (Pause.) I want you home by . . .

Get on with it!

Just drive carefully, all right, and if you're going to screw someone, use protection.

I promise.

(Stops half-shouting. Talks.) Are you going to see that Laura?

How come you remembered her name?

Because I remember things. (Taps head.) Remember your friend, Lucky. He called me "The Brain." The Brain remembers.

I think she'll be there.

What movie are you going to see at the Drive-in?

The Dirty Dozen.

Haven't you seen that?

I liked it. (What I saw.)

Well say hello to her from the Rabbi. (Scratches head.)

—Then I begin to wonder,
could my mother
have told him that she walked in on us
one summer afternoon when after
a dozen "hellos!" and trying
every door, she opened mine
and found us lying there naked—
or worse, with our bathing suits askew,
studying each other's bodies,
unable to retract our stupid grins.
On our way out she offered Laura "something cold to drink."
Laura giggled awkwardly "I don't think so."
My mother continued with her list of juices and sodas.
When I came back from walking her home
Mom said, "I think you like that Laura."
I said "I do"—and she—"she seemed rather mature."

♣

Odd. "Tell Laura I Love Her" was the song, after "Heartbreak Hotel," he hated most. Then "Teen Angel."

And what do the songs have in common?

The death of a young woman in a car crash by the railroad tracks.

He wouldn't have agreed with Poe then about the death of a beautiful woman being the perfect subject for a poem.

I hate leading questions.

You can't always get what you want.

But you're helping me put some stray pieces into place: long before he found your writing "morbid," that was the word he chose to pinpoint his horror of those songs.

"I don't want you listening to that morbid music," he'd say, entering my room in Kankakee while the wind-lashed branches beat against the windows without warning one night when I was—ten? And what was the big deal, I'd only played the song a thousand times.

You've overlooked that the songs have a strong Christian element. "Are you somewhere up above / And am I still your own true love." He hated sentiments having to do with the afterlife.

Haven't you left something out? Something that might elicit more compassion?

His hands always shook. He fumbled his fork toward his mouth. He couldn't spoon a boiled egg into his mouth without making the yolk wobble. And when I asked him why his hands were shaking he'd hold out his shaking hands, with gleaming manicured fingernails, and say "see, see, they're not shaking."

He always got egg on the corners of his mouth.

At a gravesite in the hills
in landsliding rain and mud
he was delivering a eulogy
to an impatient band of mourners—
when his knees started to knock.
He grabbed a tombstone to keep from falling.

He was doing the Charleston!

Anyway, people knew SOMETHING WAS WRONG!

And he began waiting for death.

("A whole lot of shakin' goin' on.")

(*Morse code was already tapping out orders*
back East for a replacement. . . .)

It was then he had the tests for Parkinsons
and wrote the letter in his fine antique hand
telling me he was ready to meet his maker.

He'd always said he knew only two things:
one that he was going to die,
I forget the other.

(My mother said: "Maybe performing
so many funerals made his legs
shake. It would mine.")

Come to the point.

Somehow in the process of diagnosing his cancer it was noted that he'd never had Parkinson's, merely a familial tremor—which is why his hands shook. But for the ten years he'd lived with the diagnosis he'd put his life on hold and didn't try to drastically improve his situation because he assumed that another congregation wouldn't want a late-middle-aged Rabbi with such a rapidly degenerating condition.

Strange how people want to know if they will live or die before they make certain choices.

As if that could in any way be predicted.

Yeah. Maybe it's a matter of the odds.

Which are always against odd men out.

Always?

Always. But sometimes they become men between.

14

In the Wake

Riding north on the bus after hours in cars
or in the air or airports or bus stations,

I felt almost happy for a moment
as the tires hissed over the wet highway,

I was both in the rain and protected
from it, distracted from grief

by the sensual pressure of the instant,
water beading on the glass, the darkening hills.

But how glad I was to be riding north!
Sunoco on one side, Mobil on the other.

His best friend was from Mobile.
I always wanted to go there.

He died too soon, or I left home,
I can't remember.

Two days ago my stepfather's body
was laid to rest.

Comatose, sucking air
through a respirator, I can't say

he was resting; I saw him
underground when I closed

my eyes at night and went
to bury the clock under mounds

of towels and pillows—I had not
heard it ticking so ferociously

while he lived—and it would not
quiet down. And the rain

tonight, it's not like any other,
and I wish the bus would go faster.

I saw the rain in the heavy hanging clouds.
That's a lie. Immense factories

blackening under a charcoal sky—
and rivers whose names I'll never remember.

I saw a sign reflected in my window:
Milwaukee Light.

Whenever the Chicago *White Sox*
beat the *Braves* it made his day.

The *Braves* were in Milwaukee then,
with lefty Warren Spahn and slugger Hank Aaron.

The bus company is *Peter Pan,*
and the *Peter Pan* coffee shop

was our first stop in Chicago when we drove in;
and that's where I was when,

though I didn't know it then,
he married my mother in Bermuda—

watching *Peter Pan* in New York
with my "real" father. . . .

And oh those prophetic lines,
not to grow up, never to go to school.

Never then to die! Only the living
are immortal. Like these rain clouds.

♣

The fact of death—a silence attends it;
an absence with which we're all

intimate. He's there when I close
my eyes but not when I reach out in the dark.

At his bedside I peeled back his eyelids,
rubbed his blue feet, his bloated hands,

almost screamed in his ear,
wake up, man, I'll be lonely without you,

*I'll be **ANGRY** if you don't wake up;*
and in the silence of our nearness to death—

the grinding hum of the generators
working at their limit for too long

to pump cool air in the killing heat;
the glug of him swallowing through the respirator.

He was the lightest sleeper I'd ever known;
he'd open one eye if I merely peeked into his room.

♣

AT THE BUS STATION IN SPRINGFIELD, MASSACHUSETTS

The lateness of the bus angers
a tough young woman from Montana

travelling with her toddler son.
And yet she knows the way: I can see it

in her green peaked cap,
her direct taut anger—*bus late,*

I kill the driver—boy knock over
suitcase—I kill him too.

♣

BUS BOARDED

The water bubbles on the windows
break; there is less and less outside to see . . .

And he was not even my real father.
That should put a cap on it.

It's like knowing the name of the lake
you pass never seeing it again and yet

finding it tough to forget,
that jagged square of black water

just off the highway—
that lake, and not another.

♣

Baudelaire boasted that he laughed
at funerals and wept at feasts.

Now in the bus it's only early evening;
I turn around and everyone's sleeping—

mother and son, matron and magician.
Half-awake, I stare at the tree line,

and the blessing of rain,
and I would like to lie down on the roadside

and drink and drink and roll
in the mud.

❧

Mortifying, one's presence in the face
of nature's sanguine gaze,

green whitewashing
the past. Whatever grooms

the body for the afterlife
pitches in this life like a tent

in a night encampment before
the dawn storming of the fortress.

The yellow day lilies wag
their heads at the first

touch of wind and I see what
others have always seen

in flowers, a sign marked
TRANSIENTS

that keeps them awake; see
now, as, standing catatonic

at the kitchen sink, the overhead
flourescent light strip sinks into the pitch

dark bottom of a coffee mug.
Seeing is native to us and yet

we stupefy our native sight.
Not the eye's sight.

❧

Some mourners hurl dirt stiffly on the coffin
because it seems the right thing to do.

Some hold back. The flag-draped casket honors
the first Army chaplain in the Pacific Theater,

for praying good prayers above the bodies
of the dead and of the living.

Prelude to an Afterword

Why should I feel compelled to write
        a thousand postscripts when I don't
work from life, but to hear
        the testimonials of people

who knew the rider, the "little Rabbi,"
        moves me to tears while I am here
to attend my mother who lies
        in bed with her stomach reaching

toward the sky—(where Sam talks
        calmly to his "grandpa in heaven,"
matter-of-fact celestial discourse)—
        and I listen to this Baptist preacher

and hospice worker as he crouches beside my chair
        in her hospital room talk about his work
with mourning; how difficult
        it is to get people to understand

the element of surprise-over-time . . . ;
        how he kissed the little Rabbi
the first time he met him
        and the last time he saw him

before "death took him so swiftly"
        there were no "last words"
and he was enveloped in silence,
        in absence—"the way death often

comes. . . ." I see him more clearly
    through this stranger's eyes.
I wouldn't have thought that he could help
    confirm my sense of what is real,

but this man who knew him less than two years
    feels so indebted that I allow myself
to think of the rider's life in terms of the people
    he affected, the bizarre love he could

elicit—not standard preacherly fare
    by any means but some connection
by being entirely present for others—
    promiscuously present—

meanwhile, as the nurses haul my mother
    from wheelchair to bed
why do I feel impelled to turn
    away . . . (we think we have the answers) . . .

and flash to an image of my friend caring
    for her father—bathing him?—but she
didn't come out of his penis, did she?
    or is that another wrong turning in my thought?

The hospice preacher offers a prayer.
    He holds my mother's swollen, psoriatic hand,
the arthritic clumps poling from her fingers,
    and as the dry, flaky patches blaze

in the unforgiving light, I find
    not a word to object to—except two—
"religion" and "churches." I tell him that I left home
    as soon as I could because I couldn't stand

being around the two of them; he admits he always
    felt sick "for hours afterward"

when he'd been with them together;
	it wasn't just quarreling, I have to add,

seeking absolution for my absence,
	but hatred (can't let my mother milk
the bereaved widow role). He nods—
	matter-of-factly. And sets me free.

Rider's Commentary on *Rider*

R. B. Kitaj, *The Jewish Rider,* oil on canvas, 1984–85; courtesy of Marlborough Fine Art (London) Ltd., London, England

Why did you take an epigraph from Wallace Stevens? If you had to choose an anti-Semite Eliot would have been better.

"____"

Why? You have to ask me why? See—"The Brain" remembers. You were spouting off about something Eliot had written about junipers and bones and I said, "Mark, schmuck, T. S. Eliot didn't write that—it's right out of Ezekiel—"

but don't tell me that you quoted those lines about the valley of dry bones during services.

Of course I had.

I don't think so.

So you know better than me. So you're right.

I just think I would have remembered.

Oh hell, you remembered. Well what would be wrong with an epigraph from Ezekiel, since he was your true, deep source.

It's too late; the book is written.

(Pause.)

Ezekiel's wheels and Mark's bicycles. I'll never forget the pathetic spectacle of you learning how to ride . . .

It looked worse than it was. You only saw the outside.

❧

There was only one problem—the steepness of the hill
so that the moment I got any momentum
it would become too hard to keep my balance *and*

press one pedal forward enough to get my weight
onto the other one. I fell more times
than I could have counted but was more

than a little aware that there were
witnesses: rubbernecking
hordes dragging home from Sears, Caterpillar and John

Deere, made somehow more than punily human while in
the fabulous, unimpeachable yellow
of their company vehicles, loaned to them

"at no charge for the duration"
by the invisible gods who ran these
beneficent institutions . . . ,

(fearless of the worst scenarios
even as, each night, they dug a few feet
deeper, making progress, slow but steady,

on their fallout shelters . . . which lent beauty
to the nights and weekends they might have wasted,
mowing; and uprooting dandelions . . .).

It was clear from the moment when I was airlifted
to "the Heights," that every other able bodied kid
at the advanced age of six could handle a two-wheeler;

there was no question that for the other
children it would have required massive regression,
a dip into the archaic, bicameral mind—

recapitulating the history
of the species' struggle out of the ooze
to mastery—to begin to dredge up

an image of themselves grappling so clumsily
with simple tools, handlebars and pedals,
like "lead-footed" Parnelli Jones

after another brave victory at the Indy 500
being asked—while his tires were still scorched—
who invented the wheel.

I was fine while I could ride in circles,
circumnavigating the flat patch
that, guarded by sawhorses, fronted

the prefabricated yet eternally
unfinished ranch house where idle bull-
dozers and cranes were petrifying fast.

I never rode in circles, I would not
ride without slight lurches
to the left and right,

the zig zag pattern I felt compelled
to retrace without knowing what I was
doing; and who knows but that from an aerial height

or view from the highest mound
my awkwardness might have been mistaken
for acrobatic grace!

The sight and smell of my own blood did
make me queasy; but you know
how pain is: it goes beyond itself.

I don't know what stopped the crowd
from splitting its sides, what turned
their faces ashen—a cloud blocking out

the sun's last rays, or some animal sense
of the blood—bright on my extremities;
or . . . the ruin of a good pair of jeans. . . .

Of course I would have preferred
to carry out this rite in private—
say on a rich man's sequestered driveway,

under the silent tunnel of his elms,
but what did it matter, in the end, how
I learned to get where I wanted to go.

♣

So at seven I gave Hebrew lessons and you made a bloody spectacle of yourself in public. What's past is past—but you still got a lot of facts wrong. First, that lunatics name was not Karl Angel but George Adam, and I know that while you changed some names slightly that this is a genuine mistake.

I know. But I had forgotten . . .

ADAM. And you with your morbid obsession with falling?

And when I had the idea of you wrestling with him I thought Angel was almost too good to have been "real"—and it echoed "Teen Angel."

I'm just telling you his name. Also, I was never an alcoholic, I just had two highballs—measured jiggers—

I thought you were going to say *ounces*

to relax me. My doctors approved. Third—

Can you please—please—stop counting.

I'm not counting. I'm just telling you the facts.

Don't get angry.

I'm not angry. I'm never angry. *You want me to stop counting so I'll stop counting. (Pause.) What else do you want me not to do. I don't want to do anything to annoy you. I know you're a very sensitive sort of plant.*

You're angry.

I'm not angry.

(Pause.)

But you know this talk about "angry" reminds me . . . of something . . . do you know what I'm going to say . . . ?

When Sam was little . . . ?

*And he said "I'm **going be ang-wy** . . ."*

It was so funny. That way of future tensing everything.

"*Going be . . .*"

(Sidney shakes his head rhythmically from side to side and repeats "going be" several times as if bemused.)

Tell Sam to come here.

Don't tease him.

*I'm not going to tease him. I'm just going to ask him if he's "**going** be ang-wy" . . .*

I tease him too, but he hates it. But I too love to remember the days—while you were alive—when he was always "going to" mete out all these just punishments on anyone who crossed him. And yet what made me melt was that his voice was never more sweet than when he issued threats or sang of "playing rough."

He's a delightful child. How's . . . Ma-de-laine.

She's good.

(He raises his eyebrows dramatically.)

Good. Is she still—angry?

What do you mean?

I mean she could be very snappish and disrespectful and I wonder if she still has such a short . . .

I thought you couldn't hold grudges in heaven. Watch out or you'll be demoted.

That reminds me. Do you remember your teacher Mr. White.

Who was black. Sure.

Do you remember what he used to say? "And for ***to-ma-wo.***"

To tell you the truth I've always had a problem envisioning a tomorrow. I find it hard to retain the concept of a future tense. And the word is always missing from my dictionaries.

Missing? Is there an empty space?

No. No clue that "future" ought to be a word.

Since I spent my hard-earned money on these dictionaries you owed it to me to have said something before.

"____"

Now listen. . . .

I'm trying, but my head hurts.

What's the matter?

It's my second flu this month.

Are you taking care of yourself?

Yeah. More or less.

Well don't overdo it.

Ok.

Remember moderation. And be good to your mother. She has no one else in the world.

We've been through that. Your pre-posthumous concern for her consumed our last conversation.

Yeah but she thinks you don't care for her.

She thought you didn't care for her.

She told you that?

Told me that. *Told* me that.

Is that the kind of thing I would make up?

(Silence.)

Tell Sam his Opa loves him.

I will. He loves you too.

Really? He remembers me?

He talks to you in heaven. So divest yourself of your grudges. I'd hate to have him call you one day and find that you've been sent away.

Demoted. Ok, for Sam's *sake, I'll be good.*

I detect some irony in your voice.

I detect some irony in your *voice.* (Pause.) *Are you giving him any sense of religion.*

You would have loved it. Friends encouraged us to come even though we didn't have tickets. It was Yom Kippur eve. We crept in with the crowd, he in his yellow-green Oakland A's hat and shiny turquoise Mets Jacket . . . we mounted the balcony with our friends and went to take a seat next to theirs when a woman waved a fistful of tickets in the air and threw us a stony look and said, "Excuse me, but these seats are reserved. Do you have tickets?" "Not for these seats," I lied, "but we wanted to sit with our friends." "Well I'm sorry," she said, "but I have reserved these seats." So Sam and I ran downstairs and sat—he counted—in the twelfth row. But once the Rabbi hoisted the Torah out of the ark, Sam *had to get closer* and sped down the aisle. Our friends waved from the balcony. "When he's going to take off that—that—*co*ver?" Sam asked. I had to grab him by the collar to keep him off the stage, slow his progress *into* the ark. "What if he drops it?" It was like a striptease, the way they delayed taking off the shiny turquoise raiment, with the raised, white, emblazoned letters, combined with the slowness with which they inched the Torah open to commence reading out loud. . . . I can't say we didn't stand out like two goyim, since my yarmulke had long ago exploded from the crown of my head. . . .

I don't know why you would go to an Orthodox shul.

It's not; it's conservative, funky, and conveniently across the street.

I didn't raise you to wear yarmulkahs and go around with your pockets empty—the whole point of the reform movement was to get rid of laws that were no longer necessary. To get beyond superstition. Those holiday Jews, those dalliers in the house of God, were not thinking about God or God's absence but dying to know if your little guy was or was not—a Jew!

You just say that because you loved ham and bacon.

That's not true! I ate pork maybe twice a year at most.

Twice a month.

Now you're crazy.

Once a month?

Once a year!

And didn't it always happen that a congregant happened by . . . ?

"_____"

And spread the word that "the Rabbi eats pork."

And what about you? When I think of all the times I had to bail you out. Why you owe me. . . .

I know.

Well I know too. Without me you would have ended up in reform school. They would have packed you off to Joliet. And I want to come back to something else . . . because it's a very important ethical point. (Bends back forefinger with thumb.) *Nobody who wanted to attend high holy days would have been denied entrance to my synagogue.*

Not even Karl Angel?

You know the answer to that. I still don't get a clear sense that Sam's getting any sense of religion. Remember I never forced you to go to temple . . .

Ill let that one go.

So do me a big favor!

Sidney, you know I'm not a believer, but I think it's good for the kid to be exposed to the rituals, the traditions; just as I think it's good for him to know how Hercules cleaned the Augean stables. . . .

Well isn't that ***great.***

But you know I never believed in God.

No. I didn't "know." I know you never set foot in temple after you left home, I know you screwed up your mind with cabbala—Adam Kadmon and the tree of life upside down with its roots dangling in the air—but I didn't "know. . . ." You never told me. And I never asked. Your relationship with God is your own business.

Sidney.

What?

Let's not waste time cavilling.

We're not cavilling, you're cavilling. You said I knew all along you didn't believe in God and I said how could I know when I never asked you.

I thought you wanted to crack a smile.

So tell me. I have some good ones for you too.

It's not a joke, jokes make me anxious, remember?

Yeah but that's because your . . . ***blood*** *. . . father . . . bloody Charles . . . used to say things to you and if you laughed he'd look at you with a straight face—no expression!—and say "what's so funny?" I never did that with you. Oh we laughed together, you and I. . . .*

I know. And that's why I want to tell you about this "parent conference."

Oh do I remember those . . . and that time when you were in fifth grade in Kankakee, waiting outside your classroom door when you didn't know I was there, I watched you fall into an intergalactic reverie over a leaf as it meandered toward tenebrous shadows . . . and I sent up a little prayer . . . that you would be spared the humiliation of being called on before the bell rang . . .

Don't interrupt.

I'm not interrupting. I never interrupt. But I remember that speech by Mr. . . . Gout . . . that's right . . . I could never forget . . .

> "*we got some pretty good guys*
> *and some pretty bad guys*
> *and some pretty bad good guys*
> *and some pretty good bad guys*
>
> *and you are . . .*"

I never remembered how he finished the sentence!

a pretty bad good guy—meaning you weren't a hard core criminal.

I think it was the other way around. Gout was an idiot.

He thought you thought he was an idiot. He didn't like the way you looked at him.

(Raises eyebrows. Makes "stern" face.)

Can I finish? Sam's teacher called us in to say—in solemn tones—shortly after our quarter of an hour in temple on Yom Kippur—that when she pointed to a harmonica and asked the children to write down the word Sam wrote

yarmulke

I wish I could see him.

I wish I had insisted that you come to the phone when mother first called to say that I "better get down" there. She didn't say much, and had said it often before about matters that weren't about to detonate, but she was whispering, and I should have remembered that when she

talks in that low voice

something is definitely up.

I was weak.

Why did you have to be comatose? Why did your doctor keep you on a respirator when he knew there was no hope, why prolong—this hovering . . . ? After a few days I started going into mother's workroom in the morning to unburden myself on her Brother typewriter for an hour or so. Or just to be alone. Mother was—unreachable—reaching for the phone like a lifeline.

She had "hired a woman" to help keep the house going.

There was a knock on the door. I—opened—it. And the woman said: "Your mother asked me to tell you that your stepfather is dead." I said, "Thank you." Then I asked: "Why didn't my mother tell me. How could she send you to tell me this?" She repeated her instructions.

She was on the phone in her slip and her curlers, waving me away with the violent downward movement of her arm that means, "Don't BOTHER me now because I'm TALKING (can't you see?) on the PHONE. And it's VERY important."

The calls of strangers always took priority in this house.

"How could you send a messenger?"

But of course when she hung up the phone we hugged and consoled each other. And yet my anger at her put me at a distance from my grief—.

So much between us had to be left unresolved.

That's because you—

♣

Why couldn't you come to the phone?

I was weak.

Your preferred word had been "feeble."

But that just meant I couldn't get around, and that the trip to New York had become too difficult. This was different.

I just wanted to have said—a last time—I love you.

Well I loved you. I always loved you. There was never any question about our love. Remember how I'd walk into the room and you'd say "Hands up, partner, I'm gonna keel ye-u-ew." Well now I'm dead. And the dead are untouchable.

But not unreachable.

UNIVERSITY PRESS OF NEW ENGLAND publishes books under its own imprint and is the publisher for Brandeis University Press, Brown University Press, University of Connecticut, Dartmouth College, Middlebury College Press, University of New Hampshire, University of Rhode Island, Tufts University, University of Vermont, and Wesleyan University Press.

ABOUT THE AUTHOR

Mark Rudman is Adjunct Professor in the writing programs at Columbia University and New York University, editor of the literary journal *Pequod*, and the recipient of numerous awards. His most recent book is *Diverse Voices* (1993).

LIBRARY OF CONGRESS CATALOGING-IN-PUBLICATION DATA

Rudman, Mark.
Rider / Mark Rudman.
p. cm. — (Wesleyan poetry)
ISBN 0–8195–2214–7 (cloth).—ISBN 0-8195–1217–6 (pbk.)
I. Title. II. Series.
PS3568.U329R53 1994
811′.54—dc20 93–38326